Stories That Won't Go Away

WOMEN IN VIETNAM
1959-1975

COMPILED BY
BETTY J. MERRELL AND
PRISCILLA TUNNELL

New Hope
Birmingham, Alabama

New Hope
P. O. Box 12065
Birmingham, Alabama 35202-2065

Dewey Decimal Classification: 266.0092
Subject Headings: MISSIONS—VIETNAM
                  MISSIONS, FOREIGN
                  WOMEN IN MISSIONS
                  WOMEN MISSIONARIES

Cover design and illustration by Barry Graham

ISBN: 1-56309-112-7
N954118•0695•5M1

Dedication

We dedicate the brain, brawn, emotions, and spirit that come to life on these pages to the heroic Vietnamese people who met life in its worst forms in their best manner. They met the mowing machine of death on a binge as courageously as any people could, who made their moves elsewhere through the night with unfathomable courage, innovation, and determination, and settled into new places with grace, dignity, and aplomb—or who stayed put to dig in their heels in the homeland they knew, where they opted to face the unknown on familiar soil. We offer here our dedicatory prayer. We invite all who read to pray it with us:

> Our Father, Who art in Heaven,
> Hallowed be Your Name,
> Your kingdom come in Vietnam
> As it is in Heaven.
> Give them this day their daily Bread,
> And forgive their Trespasses as they
> forgive those who Trespass against them.
> Steer them around Temptation
> And deliver them from Evil.
> For yours is the Kingdom,
> the Power,
> and the Glory,
> Forever. Amen.

Contents

Roll Call of Southern Baptist Women and Their Daughters in Vietnam: 1959-75

Preface

At varying times between 1959-75, 38 women wound their way from different parts of the United States to South Vietnam. Twenty-three of us were accompanied by husbands; fourteen were single women. It was a unique time and this was a unique line of people who marched in and out of what the world perceived as a war zone. Each of the women went there out of a sense of call and mission. Twenty-eight of our daughters lived with us. They spent their growing up years in Vietnam.

As you begin to live our experiences through the pages of this book, you can imagine what a relief it is to breathe out loud some of our best and worst times. Before you're through reading, you will have sensed our unanimity of vision that South Vietnam was a beautiful place, a wonderful place, a hard place.

In that setting, we asked the question of Psalm 37, "How shall we sing the Lord's song in a strange land?"

Some writers and speakers during the war years pointed to Vietnam as a symbol of abandonment by God, or as their proof that "there is no God." To women who lived under the canopy of God's call in Vietnam, it seemed that God chose to love South Vietnam in a hovering embrace. While man started and sustained the period of embattlement, God walked among all peoples there through the good times and the pain, the sunshine and the rain, the music and the silence. What would it have been without His Presence? We saw Him, heard Him, and felt Him there.

Because that loving God lived and breathed in us, we too loved the Vietnamese people. We would have been glad to have included North Vietnam in our expressions of love, but it was not open at the time.

The community God pulled together for this time, this place, was awesome in its depth, its love, its zeal. The spirit of urgency resulted in a dynamic bonding that enabled and encouraged us to remain faithful and hang together no matter what the circumstances. The community of faith encircled missionaries of less than ten groups, lay Christians from other nations, Americans stationed in Vietnam (civilian and military), and a growing number of Vietnamese Christians.

When the government of South Vietnam came under Communist rule April 30, 1975, missionaries and Vietnamese Christians agreed that as missionaries, we would no longer be welcome or safe within its borders. So we left, but we did not forget its people, its color, or its culture. We left some pieces of our hearts there; we've carried the other pieces—the symbols, images, and stories—with us wherever we've traveled or settled during the 20 years since our exodus.

Some missionaries were quickly reassigned to other fields; some worked with Vietnamese refugees in Southeast Asia and in the United States; some moved to other avenues of ministry. All of us yearned to tell our stories. At first, few wanted to listen. Audiences were war weary and that's what they associated with the V word.

After a while Christian people began asking to know more. As we would stand to tell of God's guidance, His help, His watchcare, His successes, and our failures, listeners would laugh, cry, then say, "You should write a book!" We would say, "But we're not writers," or "Who would read it?" or "Maybe someday," or "Yes, we should." And the dream was born! We should write a book—together. Every woman who served as a missionary—whether long-term or short-term, volunteer or career—and our daughters had stories to tell. In order to tell *the* story, we had to tell *our* stories. The dream presented itself at just the right time to release the stories during the 20th memorial year of the dramatic and traumatic days that triggered our transfers out of the country. We have participated in oral telling of them through the years. Now it is the season to offer them in concrete form to a larger audience of readers as a tribute to a time, place, people, and Presence.

We present the stories in the format in which we lived them: Divine direction, earthbound experiences, and learnings that we caught and trapped for future recall.

The 100 stories herein are but a few of those that come back to clog the pathways of our minds. They are representative of our myriad experiences as we "walked before God in the land of the living" in South Vietnam (Psalm 116:9). *They are as we've remembered them for 20 years.* They encompass the stories of those with whom we walked: Vietnamese, American, missionaries of all groups present there, and persons from many countries who volunteered or were sent. The remembrances are valid—they could have happened to anyone, anywhere, anytime.

We hope they will happen again in you as you read.

Prissy Tunnell and Betty Merrell
Collectors and Compilers

Our Entries

———

1

Are You Taking Your Children?

Mary Humphries

"Peace is what I leave with you; it is my own peace that I give you. I do not give it as the world does. Do not be worried and upset; do not be afraid" (John 14:27 TEV).

As a young girl studying missions, I memorized the Great Commission found in Matthew 28:19-20; but not until I was serving as a missionary in Vietnam did I realize that the Commission was not complete without verse 18. "All power is given unto me in heaven and in earth. Go ye therefore, and teach all nations, baptizing them in the name of the Father, and of the Son, and of the Holy Ghost: Teaching them to observe all things whatsoever I have commanded you: and, lo, I am with you alway, even unto the end of the world" (KJV). The Great Commission begins with the assurance of His power and ends with the promise of His presence. That is all we ever need in order to go where He leads.

When we began thinking about going to Vietnam, Jim was pastor of a church in Fort Worth, Texas. We had two boys, one almost eight and the other three years old, and a newborn baby girl. Jim came home one day and said, "How would you like to go to Vietnam?" The war in Vietnam was just beginning to escalate, so I thought he was joking and said, "Yeah, why not go to Timbuktu?"

Jim told me about an English-speaking church in Saigon, in existence for five years that had never had a pastor. As we prayed about it, we felt more certain that God was calling us there. People asked, "Are you taking your children? Are you taking your children into the middle of a war?" Finally, I started answering, "No, we're just going to give them away." Of course, if we went, we would take our children; we were a family and we would all stick together. However, this really began to gnaw at me, to shake my confidence, and I knew that I must get it settled with the Lord, so I went away to pray.

My prayer started something like this, "Now, Lord, I believe with all my heart that you are calling us to Vietnam, but you know the situation there. You know the danger. If we are unwisely subjecting our children to danger, don't let us go; just close the door." I left it in God's hands. I rested in Him for whatever was to follow and I had a peace about it. Well, He didn't close the doors; in fact, He opened them wide, so quickly they almost fell off their hinges. We knew without a doubt that it was His will for us to go.

While in Vietnam, I believe the greatest danger would have been to be in the wrong place at the wrong time. Even though there was fighting not very far away, we went on with daily tasks. The children mirrored our actions. If we were calm, they were calm. If we were upset and panicky, so were they.

My greatest concern was always for the safety of the children. I began to think that if anything happened to them it would be my fault. They didn't choose to come. Jim and I had made that choice; they had to follow. I spent a great deal of time praying about this and God helped me realize that my children could be killed in Fort Worth, Texas. The safest place to be was in the center of His will.

In 1968 during the Tet offensive, fighting exploded all around us. There was no safe place to run. I became frightened and I couldn't honestly tell my children, "Don't be afraid," for I was afraid myself. Kids can spot fakes and phonies instantly. I had never ever been really scared before. Now I had a terrible gnawing in the pit of my stomach and nausea was coming in stages. I could not continue like that. I had to do something. Once again I went alone to pray. I had to get it settled. I prayed it again: "Now, Lord, I believe with all my heart that it is Your will for us to be here, but You know the danger surrounding us right now. You know how scared I am and how concerned I am about our children. I think Jim and I are ready to die—if we don't have to be tortured!—but we can't make that choice for our children. Lord, You know I don't have very much faith right now, just barely a little tiny mustard seed kind of faith; but with all the faith I have, I'm asking that you remove this fear from me." Immediately, a sense of peace and calmness came over me, the kind I'd never before experienced, and I knew God was in control.

At that time, He gave me a verse which became, perhaps, my all-time favorite. It is Philippians 4:6-7 which says, "Be anxious for nothing, but in everything by prayer and supplication with thanksgiving let your requests be made known to God. And the peace of God, which surpasses all comprehension, shall guard your hearts and your minds in Christ Jesus" (NASB). I learned without a doubt that it is possible to have the peace of God which passes all understanding even in the midst of war. This peace is in no way dependent on outward circumstances, but comes from deep within us where the Spirit of Christ dwells.

4

2

Birthday

Rachel James

"The angel answered, 'God is pleased with your prayers and works of
charity, and is ready to answer you'"
(Acts 10:4b TEV).

July 1962. The day to leave North Carolina for South Vietnam had arrived.
We did not yet have visas to enter Vietnam. We were instructed to go on to
San Francisco and our visas would be there waiting for us. We boarded the
plane in Raleigh with our 3-year-old daughter, 18-month-old son, and our
newly born 8-week-old son. We flew to San Francisco to board our ship
which would take us to Hong Kong enroute to Vietnam. Upon arrival in San
Francisco, no visas were awaiting us. Instructions came to proceed to Hong
Kong and await our visas there. After three weeks aboard ship, we arrived in
Hong Kong. No visas.

We settled in at a small Chinese hotel. Sam began teaching Greek at the
Hong Kong Baptist Theological Seminary. We both started teaching English
conversation at Pui Ching Middle School.

In late August we received word from the Vietnamese consulate: "Your visa
request has been rejected." Under no circumstances could we enter Vietnam,
they confirmed. We knew God had called us to that land. We could not con-
sider giving up. Our only choice was to reapply and we did.

July went into August and August into September. Day by day we waited
and awaited word. At the beginning of October, I told Sam, "We need not
worry any longer because my birthday will be October 17. My name will be
on the missionary prayer calendar for the very first time.* Thousands of
Baptist Christians around the world will be praying on that day for our needs
to be met, though they have no idea what our needs are." We talked no more
about visas during the next two weeks of July.

On October 17 at 2:00 in the afternoon the phone rang in our hotel room.
It was the Vietnam consulate in Hong Kong. They said, "We have just received

a cablegram for you. Would you like for us to read it to you?" We tried to calmly say, *please*. It read, "Your visas have been granted. You may proceed to Vietnam at your convenience."

Some may say that this was a coincidence. We do not think so. Because Christians prayed, God answered in a specific way.

The prayer calendar is a monthly listing of Southern Baptist missionaries on their birthdays.

3
Hurry Up and Get in This House
Priscilla Tunnell

"When I lie down, I go to sleep in peace; you alone,
O Lord, keep me perfectly safe"
(Psalm 4:8 TEV).

Our crates had finally come. It was like Christmas to unpack and put things in place in our new home. We laughed at a few of the funny things that somehow had slipped past "the sensibility check" in packing, but that just added flavor to the task. "Where are we going to put all this stuff," we'd say as we stared at the menagerie.

We were settling in and looking forward to a long and exciting adventure serving the Lord in Vietnam. We would be in Da Lat for language study for quite a while before the anticipated move to Saigon. We had read everything we could find about Vietnamese history and culture as preparation. We knew that the biggest celebration of the year was coming, Tet.* The easiest way to explain Tet would be to describe it as New Year's Day, Valentine's Day, Memorial Day, Fourth of July, Labor Day, Thanksgiving Day, and Christmas all rolled into one three- or four-day event.

On Tet eve we unpacked the last box, enjoyed dinner, and decided to turn in a little early. Before going to sleep we discussed what kind of curtains we should make to hang at the windows. Just thinking of that made us sleepy enough to drift off. At midnight Gene and I simultaneously rose up out of our beds. Our feet hit the floor and on our knees we went scrambling to our son's room. We grabbed our son, Mark, out of his bed and pulled him down on the floor with us. The noise was deafening and the sky was bright as noonday. We looked for a place to hide from those bare windows. We crawled back into our bedroom on the back side of the house. In the corner we went, pulling mattress and box springs down on top of us.

For hours we heard the guns. We could hear explosions and people running, hollering. Whenever we peeked around the mattress, the sky was bright with flares. We spoke a few thoughts and questions for God under that mattress. *We just got here! We haven't done anything to help these people or tell them about You! . . . Take us, but don't let anything happen to Mark! . . . Why did you bring us here if you don't need us here!*

After those first conversations with God, I had to figure out how to get to the bathroom. Our house had been built by the French so the toilet was elevated quite a bit. Gene reminded me of this and the fact that there were no curtains at the windows. I said I had to try. As soon as I crawled into the bathroom, a loud explosion seemed to occur right outside the bathroom window. That ended that! Back to the mattress I crept.

The night seemed to double in length as we talked and prayed. Mark finally went to sleep just before dawn, about the time the noise settled down. As daylight came we inched along through the house, carefully peeking out of windows to catch a glimpse of anything that could tell us who was now in control of the city.

Mark woke up hungry. I managed to get a little something to eat while sitting on the floor of the dining room. From that vantage point we were able to see down our driveway to the street. The neighborhood was very quiet and the street was empty. Normally it was quite busy that time of day. All of a sudden Mark jumped up with excitement and yelled, "Uncle Earl!"

There stood Earl Bengs, then senior missionary in Da Lat, tall in stature, walking very nonchalantly up our driveway. Gene ran to the door, jerked it open and yelled at him, "Hurry up and get in this house." Gene pulled him in and inquired, "Why are you out walking around at a time like this?"

Earl broke into laughter as he surveyed the scene and realized what had happened. Then he told us what Tet is all about. "Everyone who has a gun (and that was almost everyone) will fire it," he said. "The soldiers celebrate by shooting off flares, throwing grenades, and the young people are all out on the streets running, yelling, and having a great time. It is quiet in the morning because they are tired, and this is family time!"

For years, we have laughed about this night. But that night it was no laughing matter. I was afraid. In fact, that is the most afraid I ever remember being in my whole life. I knew God was there. I knew He cared about me and my family. I also knew I could depend upon Him, but I was still afraid. I learned about fear that night; it gave me a point of reference for relating to and understanding when someone else is afraid.

*Tet is the Vietnamese name for the Lunar New Year period celebrated annually in most of Southeast Asia.

4

Managing the Tones
Rosalie Beck

"But in church worship I would rather speak five words that can be
understood, in order to teach others, than speak thousands
of words in strange tongues"
(1 Cor. 14:19 TEV).

In high school I studied French. In college I studied German and Dutch. I
loved languages. But nothing I had done before arriving in Vietnam in the
summer of 1973 prepared me for learning a tonal language. During training I
read about the language. I went through a series of classes on language learning. But, I had never tackled a language that depended on the tone of my voice
to translate meanings. Missionaries who live and work in lands with tonal languages earn my profoundest admiration!

The South Vietnamese language uses six tones. The word *ma* can mean six
different things, from *mother* to *ghost*, depending on which direction your
voice goes when you say the word. For example: Rondal Merrell, the missionary pastor of a church in Saigon, asked the family's helper to buy six
cucumbers for a salad. When she came back with six pineapples, he realized
that his voice had gone up instead of remaining level.

In English we often indicate a question with an upturn of the voice at the
end of a sentence. To do that in Vietnamese was deadly because the meaning
of the word at the end could completely change with the up tone. So, not only
was I assigned to learn a new vocabulary and grammar, I had to pay strict
attention to the disciplines of my voice inflections.

My most embarrassing moment came as a result of not paying attention to
the direction of my voice. I often went to the market to practice my
Vietnamese. I studied daily with Ba Khuong (Mrs. Koo-ung). The people in
the market enjoyed helping me correct my pronunciation and grammar.

On the day of my demise, I arrived at the market determined to work on
the greetings I had just learned. The Vietnamese people hold the elderly in

high esteem, and the language has a special form for addressing an old man or woman. I went up to an elderly peanut seller and addressed him in what I thought was good Vietnamese. "Most honored sir," I thought I said. He immediately went into gales of laughter. The Vietnamese usually didn't laugh in my face when I made a language mistake, so this set me aback. I was determined, however, to master this phrase.

I approached an elderly woman and thought I said, "Most honored m'am." She looked surprised, put her hands in front of her mouth and giggled loudly. I had learned that this action was a sign of amusement or embarrassment. Now I was embarrassed. Obviously, I was saying something that surprised and tickled people. I had to find out what I was saying.

The next day, as Ba Khuong and I sat studying, I cleared my throat and proceeded to recount my dilemma. She spoke no English, so it took a bit more of my Vietnamese and some pantomime for her to understand. I asked what I'd said. I repeated the phrase again and she threw her hands in front of her face and giggled! No matter how persuasive I was, she refused to explain to me what I'd said. I knew it must be bad.

That afternoon I walked to the church for a meeting with some of the young people. When I approached the building, one of the young women caught up with me and we walked together. Thao knew some English and had been around Americans for years. She understood that I really wanted to know the mistake I made in order to say it correctly. When I told her what I had said, she giggled into her hands. I thought, *Oh, no, not again!* But Thao, knowing that I was serious about my language study, led me to a dictionary and showed me what I was saying. It turned out that I was not pitching my voice low enough. I had trouble hearing and speaking the low tone, and the word translated "most honored" called for that tone. I was pitching my voice in the middle level. I was not calling the merchants "most honored" anything. I was calling them a part of a man's anatomy that isn't to be shown in public. If he does show it, he gets arrested! I was mortified. I did not want to return to the market!

As I thought about it, I knew I had to go back and correctly address the merchants I had amused so much. I "girded my loins" and returned to the market, only after Ba Khuong assured me I was now saying the word correctly. I shall never forget my embarrassment, nor shall I forget the graciousness with which they received me when I returned to correct my mistake. They knew I wanted to speak to them in their language, and I wanted to speak it correctly. This gave me an opportunity to share my reason for being in Vietnam. I told them that their lives were very important to me—so important that I must overcome great personal embarrassment to establish friendships with them.

5

Making Memories

Paulette Kellum

"I will still be joyful and glad, because the Lord God is my savior"
(Hab. 3:18 TEV).

Language study was getting old. A little something special for our family and
the Tunnell family was overdue. After dinner one night, someone said, "Fourth
of July is coming. Maybe we can go on a trip." The kids overheard our conversation and voted for it 100 percent. We all decided that a trip to Cam Ranh and
the beach would be great. So we made plans and listed all the things we would
take for this two-day trip. We weren't sure what we would find in Cam Ranh.
We had never been there, so we wanted to be prepared. We packed several cool-
ers of food, a couple of changes of clothes, toys, books, and, oh yes, all the electric appliances we would need to prepare food for the eight of us.

On the big day we all piled into the Volkswagen van and headed around
those mountain roads on our way to the beach and a Fourth of July to remember. The trip was fun, as fun as it can be with four children under the age of
six in one vehicle. We bounced up and down and slid side to side all the way
to Cam Ranh. Upon arrival we hunted till we found a motel that boasted of
electricity. It wasn't the cleanest facility in the world, but with the cleanser we
brought we could make it sanitary. We were able to get two rooms side by side.
One could hear easily what went on in the next room, so there were no secrets
between these two families.

We all seem to remember different things about the trip, but one thing is
remembered by all. The first morning we decided that we would have a nice,
big breakfast before heading for a day at the beach. Out came the electric coffee pot, the electric toaster, the electric frying pan, and some of us recall a waf-
fle iron. The kids pushed tables together and set out the plates and silverware
while the rest of us began preparing the meal. First, the coffee pot was filled
with water and coffee and then plugged in. Into a plug went the frying pan
and, in turn, sausage or bacon was placed in. Oh, the smell was great! I don't

remember what came next. Actually nothing mattered after that. We blew the fuses in the whole motel. When those on duty came to check out the situation and saw all of the electrical appliances, they decided not to even bother changing the fuses. We had blown the electricity in the whole area.*

Without electricity, our celebration was dampened. But the beach was beautiful, and we found Vietnamese restaurants, and the food was just fine. We found ways to turn the local fare into a traditional American Fourth of July feast.

All a family celebration really needs is a family.

*Electricity was a luxury for much of South Vietnam. Even where it was wired into a facility, the capacity was not up to the typical American menagerie of electrical gadgetry. Adapters and alternators were as vital as having access to the current. Electricity was such a desired luxury that some neighbors tapped into the wiring to get some of the wonderful stuff. You could be unaware until your bill came.

6

Mistakes

Betty J. Merrell

"I am most happy, then, to be proud of my weaknesses, in order to
feel the protection of Christ's power over me"
(2 Cor. 12:9b TEV).

The missionaries in language study in Da Lat decided to celebrate Christmas
with a party/fellowship for our English students. Oh, we planned and produced refreshments: home-baked Christmas cookies and red punch. We each
kept freezing ice in our refrigerators until we had enough to serve with the
punch. Ice was a luxury in South Vietnam.

We wrote the Christmas story in English and prepared stick characters for
a puppet rendition of a dramatic reading of the Christmas narrative. We
rehearsed with the students—some read the narratives while others moved
Mary, Joseph, and all supporting characters across the shelf-stage at the
prompter's nod. We practiced singing the carols—in English. All was in order
and we were ready to celebrate.

The day arrived. Missionaries and families arrived early. We warmly greet-
ed the guests at the decorated door. A chatter ran on comfortably between students and teachers. The carols were a hit. Vietnamese college students always
liked singing the Christmas carols, especially "Silent Night." When the
moment for the feature arrived, all the right students were in place behind the
curtain, just as we had performed in rehearsal. The narrators read their parts
and the characters, familiar to us but not to the movers, entered and exited the
scene as we had directed. Barely into the Mary and Joseph scene, we watched
a change-up in the story take place before our eyes. We had miscalculated.

Mistake 1: We assumed the narrators understood the script and would wait
for the right characters to appear before they read the next line. They didn't.
Their thing was to read, and read they did, tasting every English word with
delight.

Mistake 2: We assumed that those who held the behavior of the first

13

Christmas characters in their puppeted hands understood what the narrators were saying. They didn't. Their assignment was to move those actors and actresses on and off their tiny stages. And they did . . . with great glee and satisfaction.

So Mary and Joseph arrived at the inn with the shepherds while the narrator told of the fury of Herod, the king. All the characters switched roles, became very independent, strolled or hurried in and out at will, spoke words that had hitherto belonged to another key player, and plotted their own stories. The missionary prompter gave up. It was English bedlam, but the students loved it. They didn't know what we knew—that "the fruit basket" had turned over . . . and over. They exited happily from behind the curtains of their backstage debut for their first-ever curtain call. We smiled at them and grinned at each other.

Refreshments waited. It was the missionary wives' turn to beam as we stood behind the table. One after another of the students turned down our long-hoarded ice for the beverage. "No, thank you, Mrs. That's just too cold." Then many passed by our beautiful sugared cookies. "So sweet." The Vietnamese eat few sweet foods.

Mistake 3: We assumed that what was important to us was as important to the rest of the world. It was not true. Vietnamese cuisine leaned toward fruit for dessert. Few desserts were ever in evidence.

We were kind of focusing on our mistakes until a student rose to read a note from all the students. It was a thank you—in English. The ending paled the mistakes that had held our attention and moved the spotlight over to why we did all this.

The student read on . . . "And finally to our teachers; we want to say thank you for teaching us about your *faith* by your faith. You have been our best example of what faith is. We need that more than anything else you could teach us."

Well, we could celebrate after all. We had done one thing right—and it was the main thing.

Because of the Vietnamese scurry to learn English, we were blessed with open doors to the hearts and lives of thousands of Vietnam's eager and sharp young minds.

7

Send-Off

Betty J. Merrell

"Be persistent in prayer, and keep alert as you pray, giving thanks to God"
(Col. 4:2 TEV).

Christmas 1963, Lafayette, Louisiana, USA. "Don't pray sleepy-time prayers for us," we begged the roomful of pastors and wives. These had been our co-laborers in south Louisiana for four years. With one year's processing of papers, interviews, and examinations behind us, we were due to leave our church in the spring and board ship in the summer, destined for South Vietnam.

The fog of eager anticipation overpowered the massive unknowns about our next four years. The political scene in South Vietnam seemed to be the first concern of all our friends. We gave it little thought, but we knew. And because we knew, we pleaded with our colleagues, "Pray for us in your most spiritually-alert moments."

8

Slide Show

Dottie Hayes

"Give them these instructions and these teachings.
Do not let anyone look down on you because you are young, but be an
example for the believers in your speech, your conduct, your love, faith, and
purity. Until I come, give your time and effort to the public reading of the
Scriptures and to preaching and teaching.
Do not neglect the spiritual gift that is in you, which was given to you when
the prophets spoke and the elders laid their hands on you. Practice these
things and devote yourself to them, in order that your progress may be seen
by all. Watch yourself and watch your teaching.
Keep on doing these things, because if you do, you will save
both yourself and those who hear you"
(1 Tim. 4:11-16 TEV).

About two weeks after moving into our first house in Saigon and before our
curtains were hung, we looked at slides of our trip to Vietnam and family por-
traits. The living room was completely visible to the street. Soon after we
began showing the slides we heard giggling coming from outside. We opened
the door, looked out, and found our fence covered with many little
Vietnamese children enjoying the free show. Even though we tried to tell them
it was OK, they all took off running. A few minutes later we heard the same
giggling and finally got the message over to them that we would love for them
to watch our slides. Some ventured all the way up to the window.

We made many little friends that night which helped us to be accepted in
the neighborhood. I wrote my parents that if getting a crowd together was this
easy, we had it made.

Sunrise, Sunset

Beth Goad

"Lord, you are my God; I will honor you and praise your name.
You have done amazing things; you have faithfully carried out the
plans you made long ago"
(Isa. 25:1 TEV).

Easter Sunday number one in Vietnam was *"mot ngay vui-ve, sung-suong, dac-biet."* That is, it was one more special, special, *special* day! Not only was it a first for our family in Vietnam, but it launched a series of firsts for those who attended the Baptist Chapel in Da Lat.

At the Da Lat station meeting one night, we were talking about the feasibility of an Easter sunrise service. When the question of where came up, we suggested our house. We were often awed by sunrise from there, and our yard had a natural stage. The level of the entrance on the south side of the house dropped abruptly to the level of a lower entrance on the east side.

We arranged chairs on the lower level, leaving the upper level for a performance by our young people. Our youth group had translated an Easter playlet into Vietnamese. They had been diligently practicing the drama, based on Peter's great confession of faith: "Thou art the Christ, the Son of the Living God."

The young people were sure that only a few of their young friends would attend; however, 45-50 people of all ages came. And as though we had planned it, the sun put in its appearance as they arrived. Just after 6:30 A.M. the sunrise service began.

At the beginning of the service, missionary Earl Bengs had given opportunity for "popcorn" testimonies of praise to the Lord, something those young Christians had never done. I could hear Easter alleluias in the heavens as the few older Christians and the brand new ones opened their lips and praised the Lord!

Though these youth had little experience in dramatic interpretation, they were resplendent in their bathrobe costumes and burned-cork beards. I was moved to tears by their conviction in dramatizing and by the realization that most of them were relatively new believers.

Following the Easter worship experience, we invited one and all into our home. Sherry Bengs and I had prepared coffee, green tea, red tea (the nearest thing to American tea available in Da Lat), cinnamon rolls, muffins, and bananas. Green tea is commonly referred to as "Vietnamese tea." It is greenish in color and somewhat bitter. We made a discovery that morning. The Vietnamese people present said they didn't really like the green tea! Hardly anyone but the older folks drank any, but they surely liked the coffee! Everyone was in a joyful mood, and the fellowship together was sweet.

Around 8:15 in the morning, Earl herded them into the cars. It was past time for the 8:00 Bible class in English for the young people. At 9:00 we worshiped in song, prayer, and reading of the Scriptures. Following that, three girls were baptized.

That afternoon, I had an opportunity to go to the Tin Lanh (Good News) church to meet with their women's group. They had invited me to give my testimony. I wanted so very much to do the whole thing in Vietnamese, but was not yet proficient enough. A young girl who formerly taught at the language school, and who had been an exchange student in New York for one year, interpreted for me. I started in Vietnamese, Co Thao skillfully interpreted for me, and I concluded in English.

The women were very receptive, and I was thrilled to meet with them. The Vietnamese women were so attractive, so industrious, yet so feminine. Those who were Christians appeared to be the living example of the virtuous woman in Proverbs 31.

Later that afternoon, Ken went to teach an English class in the Chi Lang community and I went to youth choir for an hour. At 5:00 P.M. we loaded 23 people into the van and went to Chi Lang for our regular evening service. The young people presented their drama again. Their stage was the screened porch at the front of the building where we met for worship. The building being on the main street, people kept coming to watch—more seeds planted. Sherry commented later, "During the drama, it occurred to me that we all started the day together as the sun rose, and our time of worship will end with us together as the sun sets."

After the worship service, the missionaries all gathered at the Bengses' house for *pho*, a noodle soup which many of the Vietnamese eat for breakfast. We relived the day's events and planned what to do next. We all agreed that it was a fantastic time to be in Vietnam! Just as I thought there were no words to describe, Earl said it pretty well: "Like the sunset the Lord is just turning everything we do to gold for Him!"

10
The Call: The Response

Betty J. Merrell

"Then I heard the Lord say, 'Whom shall I send?
Who will be our messenger?' I answered, 'I will go! Send me!'"
(Isa. 6:8 TEV).

Christmastime, New Iberia, Louisiana, USA, 1962. My pastor-husband rose to lead in prayer to close the church's annual weeklong prayer vigil for needs in countries around the world. The petition was easy since it was printed on a page in the missions magazine the prayer leader had handed him. She had requested the pastor to close the sessions and he had accepted—as always.

"Today, somewhere," the prayer request read, "a pastor and his wife are trained, ready to fill a need in some overseas country. Pray that they will respond to God's call to go."

In that brief moment, Rondal D. Merrell, Sr., both presented the petition and provided the answer to it. I was in the meeting, but I did not know of his "Here I am, send me" response until lunchtime. He told me he was ready to write the mission board of our willingness to be sent—somewhere. We had discussed this off and on for more than five years. I nodded and agreed to change his response to "Here we are, send us."

11

The First Christmas

Dottie Hayes

"The Lord is good; his love is eternal and his faithfulness lasts forever" (Psalm 100:5 TEV).

Christmas was near, and we were still searching for a house. Six weeks had passed. We were anxious to move and get settled in, but houses were hard to find and expensive. At last we found a suitable one we could afford. Our new missionary friends had acted as our interpreters.

We were frantic to get settled before Christmas. Furniture to buy and a kitchen to stock. Oh yes, that was fun! My first meat purchase was wrapped in a banana leaf.

Among the myriad other things to do before we could actually take possession of the house, finding a *helper* was close to the top for me.* I needed someone to help me in the house, a special someone to take care of our baby girl. We ended up with three helpers that first year! I never really adjusted to helpers, but without them I couldn't have studied the Vietnamese language full time or found the time to absorb the culture of my newly-adopted country.

Each day we awaited news that our crates of furniture and other goods had arrived. No word came. We needed all the things in those crates, but were especially anxious for the Christmas gifts we had purchased for the children. Days passed without word. We had to do something. We wanted our first Christmas in this new place to be one the children would remember. What could we do? Well, what we could not do was speak the language. Nevertheless, we boldly went shopping on our own and bought gifts for each child. We were elated to find beautiful wrapping paper in the market to wrap each gift.

We were excited about our lovely purchases and couldn't wait to see the surprise on the children's faces come Christmas morning.

Before Christmas we had met a wonderful Christian American serviceman, Homer Long. Homer was stationed a few miles outside of Saigon. He came to visit us a few times. Our children loved him and started calling him Uncle

Homer. Homer and the children spent hours together; they soon became close enough to share many thoughts and wishes. Homer heard the boys say that they missed two big things—Paul's baseball team and American ketchup.

We were anticipating Christmas dinner with an American family we had met on the ship on the way to Vietnam, so we invited Homer to join us for a meal the day after Christmas. We all eagerly awaited Homer's visit. He arrived in grand style with a black satchel under his arm. He called the children to him and shouted, "Merry Christmas!" Then he reached in that black satchel and pulled out four beautiful bottles of American ketchup. The children were delighted beyond words. What a special and unique Christmas gift! It truly was a Christmas Day for us all to remember!

Oh yes, the crates arrived two weeks after Christmas, so we just celebrated again!

*Helper *was a term used by missionaries to describe the person paid to assist in the home, to free time for missionaries to invest in the Vietnamese people.*

12

The Test

Priscilla Compher

"And so I walk in the presence of the Lord in the world of the living" (Psalm 116:9 TEV).

In June 1974, we returned to Qui Nhon for what we hoped would be a four-year term there. We had left our twin sons in Huntsville, Alabama, to live with my sister and her family. They were young teenagers then, and we sensed their need for more social life than what we felt Qui Nhon could offer them. Kathy was ten and Robby was six months big!

Like Paul, we had received word of problems in the churches while we'd been gone. The two short-term missionaries who had worked in the churches during our furlough had been transferred to other assignments. The Vietnam Baptist Mission was not sure that we should return to Qui Nhon. Yet we felt God's call there; we wanted to return. The Mission approved.

Apprehensively, we flew back to Qui Nhon on the familiar DC-3. We landed at the airfield, and Bob walked to our house to get the car for us. Before we could get out of the car, we were surrounded by the women who lived along the sandy street at the back of our house. "We came to see the new baby!" they exclaimed amid their broad, warm smiles. After all had touched him to their satisfaction, they kept asking, "What are you feeding him?" (They meant, what formula are you using? Though most Vietnamese mothers breast-feed their babies, they had heard that most mothers from the West did not.) I replied, "I am breast feeding Robby," but they either couldn't understand or couldn't believe. Suddenly one elderly woman decided to clear the confusion. She grabbed a breast, then turned to the women and said, "It is full of milk; she is breast feeding the baby."

Soon our apprehensions ceased. We were received as neighbors, accepted for the second go-around. Actually, we were received more openly by the Vietnamese in Qui Nhon this time than previously. The American military, except for intelligence personnel, had gone. Local authorities no longer kept us under surveillance, and there is something about a foreigner's return that puts a trust in place.

13

Trials of a Rookie

Beth Goad

"God says, 'I will save those who love me and will
protect those who acknowledge me as Lord. When they call to me,
I will answer them; when they are in trouble, I will be with them.
I will rescue them and honor them'"
(Psalm 91:14-15 TEV).

Sunday, September 9, 1973, was one of *those* days which, reported in all honesty and candor during furlough year, would not advance the cause of missions. I can laugh about it now, but at the time it was not at all funny to this missionary who had been in her new country about three months.

The senior missionary couple, Earl and Sherry Bengs, and our family were the only missionaries in the Da Lat Mission station at that time. The preceding Wednesday, Earl and Sherry had taken their five children to Singapore to enroll the two older sons in school for the semester. Ordinarily on Sunday mornings, Earl preached and Sherry played the piano for services in the chapel. Usually evening service was held in the suburb of Chi Lang, where Vietnamese Pastor Huy preached, and Sherry again played.

We had rejoiced the preceding week when our Vietnamese Christians took full responsibility for planning the service and securing persons to fill the places of responsibility in the absence of the Bengses. Sherry had made arrangements for the music. I was to play the piano for the song service; a Vietnamese teenager, one of Sherry's piano students, was to play the offertory; and another young woman was to lead the music. As the young woman and I talked about the songs, I suggested that she select them because she knew which hymns the congregation knew. She agreed, and said she would announce the hymns, but not lead them; everyone would just follow the piano.

The piano faced the wall so the congregation was at my back. Furthermore, the hymns were all written in Vietnamese. Had it not been for the English title written underneath, I would truly have been sunk, for often the rhythm of the music had been altered slightly to accommodate the Vietnamese words. Also, the service was conducted entirely in Vietnamese.

As the service began, Pastor Huy, whom I had not met before, took charge. I was playing the piano, desperately trying to stay at the proper place at the proper time, all the while sneaking surreptitious glances over my shoulder to make sure I was doing the correct thing, since the words gave me no clue at this stage of my language learning.

When the time for the offering came, I moved from the piano bench so the girl could play the offertory. Following that, Pastor Huy picked up a hymnal and walked back to converse with the young woman who had selected the hymns. Thinking that it was time for the third hymn, I remounted the piano bench and proceeded with a snappy introduction. A moment later, Pastor Huy was behind me, saying, with pure Oriental politeness, "When we are ready to sing again, I'll tell you." Oh, brother! Had only the earth opened and swallowed me, or Gabriel called me home! Anything would have been welcome!

The evening service was act 2 of *The Blunders of Co Beth* (Miss Beth). Same preacher, same hymnbook, different church, and one interesting variation: a pump organ! I hadn't been to this church before, so I didn't know how the organ was supposed to sound. I have played any number of pump organs before, and they always remind me of the movie *Snow White and the Seven Dwarfs*. But whoever designed this organ had the dwarfs in mind, not Snow White . . . or me.

The keyboard of this one was abbreviated, as was its height. And it was the height, or lack of it, that did me in! When I got my feet into place on the pedals to pump, which was accomplished only by having the chair back several feet, my knees were rubbing on the wooden part under the keys. This particular organ was definitely in respiratory distress—asthma, emphysema, something terrible, I'm sure.

I didn't dare think of how I must look—back far enough to get my feet on the pedals and I could scarcely reach the keyboard; reach the keyboard and I was too close to get my long legs under the thing. Each pump was accompanied by two flaps and a wheeze, with various squeaks thrown in for good measure. The sound was just awful! I kept wondering, *Is this thing supposed to sound this way or are my big Western feet mortally wounding it? Surely sounds as though it is suffering agony.* I kept trying to catch Ken's eye for some indication as to whether it was supposed to sound the way it did, but my loving spouse was staring intently at the ceiling!

No rescue. No relief—except my own when the service came to an end.

14

Uncle Dan Whitt

Dottie Hayes

"For we remember before our God and Father how you put your
faith into practice, how your love made you work so hard, and
how your hope in our Lord Jesus Christ is firm"
(1 Thess. 1:3 TEV).

In 1958 Herman and I with our two small sons (and expecting our third child)
worked in a happy pastorate in McComb, Mississippi. Our church was very
missions-minded with a strong supportive women's group. We expected to
stay in McComb the rest of our lives as we felt very fulfilled and secure. That
summer the church sent us to a denominational assembly and we chose
Foreign Missions Week so we could bring back some exciting missions knowledge to our church. God had other plans.

In every session we heard missionaries tell of their experiences. Each
speaker made a strong plea for more missionaries to come and help. Never in
our wildest dreams had we thought God might use us in another land.
However, by the end of the week we began to feel strongly moved that God
might be calling us into missions work. During the week we also heard a
report that plans were being made to enter South Vietnam whenever a young
pastor and his wife were available to go.

This plea hung heavy on our hearts. In the last service of the week, a strong
plea was made for young pastors who had completed seminary. We surrendered to God's call to serve overseas that night. We left that week with great
excitement, praying we might be the ones chosen to go to South Vietnam.

After a process of several months, we were appointed to South Vietnam.
Our appointment was announced in several state papers, one of which was the
Baptist Standard of Texas. A Baptist pastor's wife in Mount Vernon, Texas, read
the article and immediately wrote us about her son, Dan Whitt, stationed in
Saigon with the US Army. She said he was a wonderful Christian and would
be excited to know of our appointment in South Vietnam and might be able

to be of help to us. We were very glad to get this news as we would be the first Baptist missionaries in Vietnam. We would not have any missionaries to call on for information and advice. Dan would become our source, and what a good source he was. One of our last letters from Dan told us he would be at the airport to greet us. We could hardly wait! He wrote to us about the American School in Saigon where our boys could attend. He told us of the Christian and Missionary Alliance guest house in Saigon and that he was making temporary arrangements for our stay there.

Much preparation and many sad good-byes remained before we would be on our way. Now we were five, having added a precious baby girl we named Hope. The anticipation of all God had in store for us was exciting beyond words. All the fears that made it hard to surrender to God's call suddenly seemed to be gone. We knew without any doubt that God would keep His promise—to be with us all the way.

We began our long journey by train from Lake Charles, Louisiana. Many friends from our church came to bid us farewell at 2:00 A.M. We arrived in beautiful San Francisco after three days of travel. We managed some sightseeing and enjoyed a memorable Chinese dinner.

Soon came the day we boarded the *President Wilson* and sailed for Hong Kong. What an experience! The food was heavenly and we each gained several pounds. The boys enjoyed the children's activities and they learned to swim. In spite of encounters with three typhoons, we would all gladly do it again.

Before leaving the States, Herman was told he would keep the financial books in the double-entry system in two currencies. What a shock! Herman had never had a day of bookkeeping or accounting. This became one of our main prayer concerns. We knew the importance of keeping an accurate account of every penny given for our work. Herman began his own personal study, getting help from a sister-in-law and buying simple books on bookkeeping to study on the ship. However, he soon realized he needed more help than that, and our prayers intensified.

After 21 days on the ship we arrived in busy Hong Kong. Our days with missionaries in Hong Kong were uplifting and were remembered long after our arrival in Vietnam.

At last we were flying to Saigon. We had read that Saigon was known as the "Paris of the Orient," and we were all eager to see what that meant. We arrived on November 1, 1959. After what seemed to be the longest part of our entire trip, the plane landed. There was Dan waiting to greet us. We loved him from the moment we met him. Even 10-month-old Hope went to his open arms and gave him a big hug. The boys thought he was rather *neat* also.

Dan took the children and me into the airport while Herman took care of our luggage. After a cool refreshing *xa-xi* soda, we sat at a small table and began to talk. At one point in the conversation Dan asked, "How do you begin Baptist work in a country like Vietnam so steeped in Buddhism?" I said, "I'm not sure, but we were told three things to do as soon as possible. One—find a house and get settled. Two—get the boys in school. Three—begin learning the language." Then I said, "Dan, Herman and I have added a fourth—to set up the financial books for our new Baptist Mission and Herman doesn't have any idea what to do." Dan looked at me with the most beautiful smile and said, "I am an accountant and I will help Herman set up those books before my tour is up the end of February." What an affirmation from God! We knew God had sent this wonderful Christian man to Vietnam.

Dan took us to the Christian and Missionary Alliance guest house. This turned out to be a most rewarding time for us as we fellowshiped with the Christian and Missionary Alliance missionaries, some of whom had served in Vietnam for many years. These colaborers in the Lord served as our interpreters when we began our long search for suitable housing. Others introduced me to the Saigon market and the secrets of bargaining. We began a beautiful relationship with the Christian and Missionary Alliance that continued throughout the years Baptists served in Vietnam.

We will forever be grateful for Dan and the many others like him who came to Vietnam because of war but made a great and lasting contribution in spreading Christianity in that needy land. And also in bringing a taste of our homeland to missionary families and allowing our children to call them *uncles*.

15

Welcome to Vietnam

Beth Goad

"Leave all your worries with him, because he cares for you"
(1 Peter 5:7 TEV).

Our very first day in Vietnam, Saturday, June 23, 1973, God proved His care and goodness to me, and confirmed that we were exactly where He wanted us to be.

We arrived in Saigon at noon, disembarked, and began the slow, slow movement through customs. There were three lines, none of which seemed marked appropriately for us, so we just got in line. While standing there, we noticed an American (we supposed it was Sam Longbottom, acting business administrator for the Mission) across the way waving us into the line to our left. "Official Passports Military."

As we stood there I noticed what looked like my gray suitcase over to the far left, already through customs alongside two brown ones. Near the baggage were two men: one appeared to be a porter, wearing an airport badge; the other was an Asian man in an orange shirt. I kept watching that bag, and commented to my husband that it surely looked like mine. Ken tried to reassure me that it probably only *looked* like mine. But I knew better!

Trying to be the submissive wife, I meekly mumbled agreement all the while thinking, "Men! That suitcase and I have been together since high school. I *know* it is mine!" And then I watched helplessly as the man carried my bag into the crowd and disappeared. I didn't know what to do! I wanted to scream, "Stop! Thief!" but that seemed a rather bad way for the new missionary to relate to her new country. We knew none of the other missionary families, and at that moment saw no one with a Western face to call on for help. I felt sick! Weak and shaky. I would have loved to just sit down and cry!

We had been two weeks in transit; that suitcase had been packed and repacked so many times. I couldn't recall exactly what it contained, but to the best of my recollection, it held most of daughter Stephanie's clothing, and some of mine.

Immediately, I was reminded of Susie Lockard's words during our time of missionary orientation, "There will be times when you will find much comfort in the fact that God has called you to your place of service." I prayed, "Lord, You have done miracles for us before. If that *was* our suitcase, please get it back to us, or grant us the grace to do without whatever was in it."

We finally made it to the baggage claim area, where our luggage and a large brown suitcase that was not ours was all that remained. Everything was accounted for, except for the gray bag. Ken sheepishly admitted, "Your suitcase is not here." Incredulously, I retorted, "Well, did you really expect it to be? I told you that was my suitcase!" So much for the submissive wife.

By this time our two children were in tears and an animated discussion had begun among several stewardesses. Ken took one of them over to Sam and got him in the discussion also. The China Airlines officials kept telling us that our bag was probably still on board and bound for Thailand. They took a complete description of it, so it could be returned. All the while, I kept telling them that the bag had been carried out of the airport by a man in an orange shirt. Though I kept up a nonstop internal pleading with the Lord, I really thought that suitcase was gone forever!

We completed the process, and rather wearily proceeded outside, where some of our Mission family waited—Herman, Dottie, and Hope Hayes; Sam Longbottom (whose wife was with their son who was hospitalized in Hong Kong); Ron and Betty Merrell; Olive Allen; and Bill, Audrey, Nancy, and John Roberson. Pictures were made and much joking, laughing, handshaking, and hugging took place. Herman and Dottie had been assigned to care for us, and they took us to the apartment in the Mission office building where we would be staying.

My perspective began to improve as we bowed for prayer before lunch. Herman thanked God for our arrival, and I thought, *Lord, how can I be upset over a suitcase full of nonessentials when You have brought the four of us safely to the other side of the world?* Herman prayed that we might hear about Stephanie's suitcase before the day was over; and I was very aware that Herman, Dottie, Hope, and Sam each confidently believed that our suitcase would be returned. He prayed that Marian and Sam's son would soon recover, and I thought, *Lord, forgive me for being upset over luggage when Sam's son is very ill. Help me to pray believing that You want my suitcase returned, that You want me happy in spite of all that goes wrong, not reluctantly dragging into service for You!*

Around 2:30 P.M. we received word from China Airlines that our suitcase was in their downtown Saigon office where we could pick it up immediately. Again, I wanted to cry . . . for joy that the lost was found, and for shame that I had prayed, but couldn't wholly believe that God cared about my lost luggage. Even then, Satan quickly jumped in to plant doubt: "What if the suitcase has been opened, and everything of value removed?"

Dottie took us downtown to get it, and once back at the apartment, we realized the suitcase was still locked. It had not even been opened for customs inspection. It had been taken by mistake along with the luggage of a couple under diplomatic immunity. The large brown bag left with our luggage belonged to them.

That experience set the tone for our entire term of service. We already knew that our heavenly Father watched over sparrows. We learned that He cares about lost things, even little things. A God Who cared about suitcases could take care of any situation we would face. Our family never forgot that.

Our Everydays

1

All for a Bag of Cookies

Priscilla Tunnell

"So then, as often as we have the chance, we should do good to everyone,
and especially to those who belong to our family in the faith"
(Gal. 6:10 TEV).

"I want to take some cookies to Andy's tonight when we go to dinner. Can we
please walk to the market and get some?" Mark, our six-year-old son, delighted in finding excuses to go to the market. When we first arrived in the country he didn't like the market. He couldn't understand anything, he didn't like
the odor, and he didn't like people trying to feel his blond hair. But as the years
went by, he realized that the market could be fun, and he had some friends in
the big market that was only a few blocks from our house. Andy Wright, a
two-year missionary, had invited us for dinner and Mark really liked him so I
felt the request was legitimate. So off we went hand-in-hand.

We shopped around, talked to some friends, bought some cookies and a
big hand of bananas. Time ticked along and we needed to get home to clean
up to go to dinner. Being invited to the home of a single, male missionary for
a meal was something new, something special.

We held hands as we walked, not so much out of love but for safety. Rules
of the road were not always in existence and I felt better having Mark's hand
in mine. About a half a block from where our street began, Mark realized that
we were almost home and joyfully pulled away from me and began running
toward the house. I yelled as I saw Mark sailing through the air having been
set to flight by a motorcycle.

I knew better. I had been taught better, but I grabbed him up and went running home screaming all the way for Gene, my husband, to open the door.
When he did, I thrust Mark into his arms and went running back to the scene
of the accident. Out of the corner of my eye as I ran with Mark, I had seen a
policeman stop. He had been behind the motorcycle.

The policeman had the motorcycle driver face down on the dirty, unpaved street and was cuffing him. I asked the policeman what he planned to do with the man. He said, "He has hit a child and I am taking him to jail." I knew that the man was in trouble.* Not only had he hit a child, but he had hit a foreign child, an American child. I told the policeman, "Uncuff the man and let him go. It was not his fault. My son ran out in front of him and he could not stop." The crowd that had gathered suddenly grew very quiet and the policeman looked at me with a question on his face. I began to wonder, *Did I say the wrong words, did he not understand what I said?* I repeated the words very slowly being careful to say them correctly.

Slowly the policeman uncuffed the man and asked me if I was sure about what I was doing. I assured him that I was and that he would not be in trouble for letting the driver go free.

It was then that the driver asked me, "Why did you do that for me?"

There on that street with the crowd gathered around I explained to the man why I was in Vietnam. I told him about God, about Jesus, and invited him to come to our church. I did not have any literature with me but I told him along with everyone else where to find the closest church. I then voiced a simple prayer for the driver and for Mark and ran home.

Gene had cleaned Mark up as best he could, and we left for the hospital for quite a few stitches. Mark was crying still, but not for his hurts. He was upset because all of the cookies for Andy were ruined.

After stitches on his head, dressings on both arms and legs, an x-ray, and a shot, we were once again on our way to Andy's with a detour by the cookie stall.

Every day is different. Every day we have the opportunity to minister. Every day we have a choice. Every day we are called on to be God's people.

Accidents in a foreign country can be costly, especially in countries where inhabitants are living under their national poverty level—that means levels lower than the American poverty level. Rarely would an accident not be used to gain dollars. Sometimes they were set up. Thus, the action taken by Prissy Tunnell would be in stark contrast to normal procedure. But then Jesus always calls forth abnormal behavior in normal followers. It leaves its mark, indelibly.

2
A Loo, a Cot, and a What?

Rosalie Beck

"The mountains and hills will burst into singing, and the trees will shout for joy" (Isa. 55:12*b* TEV).

One of the joys of missionary service is meeting other believers from around the world. In Vietnam, hundreds of Westerners served in medical and ministry capacities, and many of them were committed followers of Jesus Christ. In the coastal city of Qui Nhon, great need existed. A population of more than 250,000 people lived in what was said to be the most economically impoverished part of South Vietnam. There, many European experts helped train the Vietnamese people in medical and social ministry techniques.

The New Zealand surgical teams consisted of a large staff of doctors, nurses, and technicians who worked at the Province Hospital in Qui Nhon. Most of the Kiwis (people from New Zealand) completed their mandatory two years of public service assigned by the New Zealand government to Vietnam.

Linda Pegram and I were the only Baptist missionaries in the city for 1973 and part of 1974. Three churches, two kindergartens, and a sewing school kept us scooting. When we needed a break, we sometimes sought the company of one of the New Zealand surgical teams. Nurse Jesse Waugh and pediatrician Margaret Neeve provided needed spiritual care and support. Jesse's faith background was Assembly of God and Margaret's was Church of England. Together, we all formed parts of the loving and vibrant body of Christ.

Language difficulties obviously existed between the Vietnamese people for short-termers like myself, but I did not expect to encounter language problems with English-speaking friends like Margaret and Jesse. I discovered the barrier when Jesse invited Linda and me to visit her *hooch*. Linda didn't bat an eye and accepted the invitation. I, on the other hand, thought Jesse said *pooch*, and I wasn't that thrilled with meeting Jesse's dog. When Jesse understood my misunderstanding, she explained that *hooch* is the New Zealand term for living

35

quarters. At Jesse's *hooch*, we shared prayer and Bible study. After several soft drinks and glasses of tea, I asked Jesse for directions to her *john*. She just looked at me. I thought I had slurred my speech, so I repeated the request. Again, she stared and said something about "no Johns living in the compound." Linda started laughing. She explained that I needed to find the bathroom. Jesse answered, "Oh, you mean the *loo*." So, for language lessons for the day, I had learned that the *place where you live* is a *hooch*! And the *john* is a *loo*!

Save the Children Fund operated a children's hospital in Qui Nhon. They staffed it with British doctors and nurses. Betty Millar, a Welsh nurse, became a friend. She introduced me to the wonders of mutton cooked Welsh-style, and I introduced her to American English vernacular. When she accepted our invitation to supper one night, I realized we did not yet have napkins on the table. "Oops," I said, "I forgot the napkins." Betty looked real puzzled, or maybe shocked is a better word. When I laid a paper napkin by her plate, she broke into a smile. "Oh, *serviette*," she acknowledged. Linda and I darted looks at each other, then at Betty. "In British English, a napkin is what you put on a baby. (A *diaper*!) I was thinking, *They have very strange customs if they use diapers at dinner.*"

Language lesson for that day: a *diaper* is a *napkin*, and a *table napkin* is a *serviette*.

When resident missionaries Bob and Priscilla Compher went to the US for furlough in 1973-74, Linda occupied their home. I lived in an apartment next door. On a weekend when we were expecting four guests, we needed more beds. Betty arrived and I asked if she had a cot we could borrow. "No problem," she smiled, "I have plenty of cots. How long does it need to be?"

"Well, one (guest) is over six feet tall," I prompted. Betty's mouth fell open.

"You plan to put him in a cot? How old is he?" she kept on.

I looked at Linda. We both guessed late 20s or early 30s.

"We may have a communications problem here," Betty said. "Are you asking me for a baby's crib? That's a *cot*. Maybe what you're wanting is a *camp bed*?"

The language lesson for that day: *cot* equals *crib*, and *camp bed* equals *cot*.

I considered these people family. The mutual support from one to the other when we took a break from our work with the Vietnamese people was side benefits we had not been promised, nor did we dream of such.

3

A Move

Betty J. Merrell

"Whoever goes to the Lord for safety, . . . can say to him,
'You are my defender and protector'"
(Psalm 91:1-2 TEV).

Spring 1966, Banmethuot, South Vietnam. With the formal period of language study behind us, we searched for a way to move to Da Nang, the city selected as our next residence. Roads to Da Nang were cut off or controlled by Vietcong. An "R-and-R" (rest and recreation) weekend brought an army pilot to Da Lat, where he inquired about missionaries. His visit to our home was an answer to prayer. He found a way for us to move by helicopter. We waited for weeks for a lull between major military operations that would free a helicopter for our move.

One morning Ron declared, "They will never come." A short time later we heard the whirs overhead. "Not ours," he said, revealing the mental fatigue of waiting. Nevertheless, soon we grabbed the van keys and took off to the military airstrip.

Not one, but two helicopters had arrived! The pilots eased their big birds down onto the runway. One pilot walked toward our car. "We are looking for a Rondal Merrell—a missionary. Know where we could find him?" he asked. Did we ever!

A couple of hours later, the four of us joined our crated furniture in one of the two huge-bellied wonders. I chose the one with the piano. We were soon skirting the rugged terrain of Vietnam's highlands.

A routine check stop in Banmethuot revealed trouble. The pilot stuck his head in the open doorway and said, "We have a very worn bearing. In a few minutes we would have plummeted straight-as-an-arrow down into the unknowns of these peaks and valleys. You will need to move to the other chopper. They will repair this one and bring it on later." Once we were in the air again, I calculated the time in the US. It was time for Sunday evening worship services. Our friends, family, and churches were praying again.

4

Angel on Assignment

Audrey Roberson

"Remember to welcome strangers in your homes.
There were some who did that and welcomed angels without knowing it"
(Heb. 13:2 TEV).

When I was 16 years old, God called me to be a missionary. Twenty years later God called my husband, Bill, to go as a missionary to Vietnam. God sent us on a mission and knowing that became a continuing source of strength during the difficult experiences which came our way.

Upon our arrival in Saigon on March 13, 1960, we began our adjustments to many new ways. One of the biggest was having a helper in our household.

While tiptoeing through the first week in our new country, a Vietnamese woman about my age came seeking work as a housekeeper. Using an interpreter for the interview, I hired her on the spot.

To my knowledge Nguyen Thi Hanh never had any sense of call to do what she did for us during those early years in Vietnam. I am convinced, however, that God sent her to help us through those crucial years of service.

Chi Hanh, "our respected sister," as we called her, had two daughters still in their teens. Somewhat shorter in stature than I, she looked very much like other South Vietnamese women. As I looked into her face that day, I thought I saw character and strength. She also appeared healthy, agile, and strong. She understood little English, and could neither read nor write her own language. I sensed, however, that she was bright and intelligent. From the outset, I felt I had not only met the woman who was to be our helper, but a person who would be my friend for life. The years which followed proved my first impressions were correct, and she proved to be impeccably honest and loyal.

Chi Hanh had never worked as a cook, but she knew how to prepare many of the delicious Vietnamese dishes—which we remember longingly. I started teaching her our favorite American recipes. I wrote out the recipes; she memorized them. With time, she even improved on some of our favorites.

One of the most important tasks awaiting new missionaries is to learn the language! The woman that God sent us to help in the house taught me more household talk than all of my paid teachers. The two of us could work together for hours on projects in the kitchen or house, using sign language or swapping the English words she knew with the Vietnamese words I had learned in my formal studies.

Shortly after she came to work with us, Chi Hanh's older daughter, Theo, came to the age that she could work as her mother's assistant with the household chores. Chi Hanh would go to the market, buy baskets full of fresh groceries, meats, and household supplies. When she came home, she would recite from memory the cost of each item for Theo to write down to account for every *dong* (the currency of Vietnam) she spent.

When we hired Chi Hanh as cook and housekeeper, little did we realize she would become our tutor in Vietnamese culture, customs, and traditions. Each new day brought a fresh dilemma related to the culture in our new home. Repeatedly, she stepped in with her gift of discernment. She cautioned us about anyone she sensed might have ulterior motives in cultivating our friendships or in transacting business. Her insight and wisdom often averted problems.

How do I explain how Chi Hanh loved us? She loved our children and helped us keep them busy in an environment minus playground or television.

With unusual depth, Chi Hanh respected what we were doing in our witness and work as missionaries. Though her background was ancestor worship, repeatedly and with vigor she helped us arrange rooms and chairs for Bible study and worship. We entertained many people in our home; she prepared the meals or refreshments with pride and delight, whether for Americans or Vietnamese. After she embraced Christ as her Savior, she attended our worship meetings and helped in our missionary activities with an even deeper interest.

Chi Hanh's most difficult challenge came when we asked her to move with us in 1962 from Saigon to Nha Trang about 300 miles away. We had received a Mission assignment to begin churches in that area. That move was more difficult for her and her two daughters than was our move from North Carolina to Saigon. Later, however, she moved again with us, a change that took her farther north to Da Nang. Across the years and furloughs we lived in several cities in South Vietnam. Though Chi Hanh did not go with us to all our assignments, we always kept in touch.

In August 1970, I was told I must have a radical mastectomy. The US Army hospital would handle the surgery. Upon my return to our house in Saigon, Bill had to take our older children to Singapore to continue their schooling. Although Chi Hanh had other employment at that time, she came every night to stay with me and our small son. During that mission of mercy, she baked cookies for a meeting of missionaries scheduled at our house while I was recuperating.

I have often said, "Chi Hanh would have been willing to lay down her life for me if the circumstances required it." Fortunately that need never occurred, though I can tell you there were times when the possibility wasn't too remote. To me and my family, Chi Hanh was an angel on assignment to us. We were sent by God to share the gospel among the Vietnamese people; she was sent by God to help us.

5

Boomerang Joy

Barbara Lassiter

"The joy that the Lord gives you will make you strong"
(Neh. 8:10*b* TEV).

Bich Lien was a 24-year-old, boisterous, joyous, Vietnamese girl. She loved to play and was sometimes *a little crazy*. She had been our helper for the previous year of language study. She loved our son Anthony very much and took good care of him while we were at school. She loved dressing up and going to the market to bargain for the best food prices. She would try to outdo the missionaries in getting the lowest price.

The war in Vietnam had taken its toll on Bich Lien's family. Her parents were part of the royal family in North Vietnam. They were killed in the Communist Tet offensive in 1968. Her brother and sister were her only living relatives, and following the Vietnamese custom her older brother handled family matters. Out of the hardships in her life she had woven a determination to take care of herself.

As Bich Lien helped care for Anthony and the house, she and I became good friends. We shared our lives through things we did together. She spoke no English, but we found ways to express love through our hands, faces, eyes, tears, and laughs. We learned to give to each other and to receive from each other.

On the afternoon of January 1, 1975, the sun streamed in through the dining room window. The sun beamed upon the table where we sat. We lived in the hill country of Vietnam in the beautiful town of Da Lat. We were in language school. The year and the day had started about the same as the days of the previous year. I had invited missionary Joe Turman to help me with a presentation of the claims of Jesus Christ in simple Vietnamese and pictures. As we began to flip through the chart and share, Bich Lien, who was not known for her shyness, stepped into the room. She had been listening and wanted to hear more.

Soon she joined us. As she heard the gospel in word and picture, she expressed excitement about the possibility of forgiveness of her sin and becoming the daughter of a King. Joe asked her to write a list representing her sins and then he burned the list before her eyes. He said, "That's what God thinks of your sin. He has forgiven them. Now He sees you through the blood of His Son, Jesus—redeemed." As she watched the list burn, her eyes got very big. She grabbed my hand, then ran out of the house, down the street shouting, "I'm the daughter of a King, I'm the daughter of a King." She couldn't wait to tell everyone. Coming from the royal family, it was such a joy to think her heavenly Father was the King! Now we could walk together in the Lord and be changed to be more like Him.

In the following weeks we moved to Saigon to continue language study and begin our work. Jim was the radio and TV technician for the Mission. Bich Lien moved with us and continued to help us with the house and Anthony.

During February and March, Vietnam quickly began falling into Communist hands. Looking back, I can see how the Lord took special care of us during this very difficult and confusing time. Bich Lien was a constant source of strength and joy as we shared Christ together in a new way. Jim and I had planned to leave Vietnam two days after Easter. We had a week and a few days left. It had been a particularly hard decision and I prayed, "Lord, I need a personal word from you so I can make it through with assurance of Your presence." I was concerned about Anthony and having to leave suddenly or quickly. On Palm Sunday, the Lord gave me a promise in Isaiah 52:11-12. "Depart, depart, go out thence, touch no unclean thing; go out from the midst of her, purify yourselves, you who bear the vessels of the Lord. For you shall not go out in haste, and you shall not go in flight, for the Lord will go before you, and the God of Israel will be your rear guard" (RSV). I received and kept His peace.

That final week was very tense and confusing as we prepared to leave South Vietnam. I spent my time practicing the piano accompaniment for the Easter music and for a concert with missionary Prissy Tunnell. I talked with Bich Lien about heaven and the hope we had of meeting again some day.

One of my teachers came by the house to tell me of her husband's death and to take me to the tailor who would sew matching Vietnamese dresses for Easter. She was on her way south to be with her father, a pastor in My Tho.

I wondered what I should put in the suitcases. While I wandered around, Gene Tunnell had gone north to visit our pastors and hadn't been heard from. He finally came home on the Saturday night before Easter. His safety and his reports left us with a mix of relief and remorse, rejoicing and mourning. Emotions were extreme, and yet in it all the peace of God for me personally couldn't compare with anything I'd ever experienced.

On Easter Sunday Prissy sang "the marketplace is empty, no more traffic in the streets . . . the King is coming." Everyone cried and sensed the seriousness of the hour. We were reminded again of Christ's sufferings for us.

That evening one of the songs in our special music said it all as we heard Jesus' words again, "Father, forgive them for they know not what they do."

Later still on that night, we all agreed that the missionary women and children should leave immediately because of the danger. Then we were out.

Looking back, as we walked away from the airport gate, Bich Lien pointed to the sky. We were on our way to the Philippines.

It had been only one year and a few months since we first came to our "uttermost part of the earth." En route to Vietnam, we had stopped off in Jerusalem where I had grown up. My parents' church prayed for us and sent us from Jerusalem to the "uttermost." My mind flooded with memories of disappointments, joys, life. It seemed as though we had lived a lifetime in 15 short months.

In the process of waiting in Manila, we found a man going back into Vietnam. I told him, "Put Bich Lien in your suitcase and get her out of danger." To my surprise he did! I was at the hotel in Manila when the phone rang. Jim was calling from Clark Air Force Base. He was helping refugees get from plane to plane when he heard someone shout his name in the crowds of those running off one of the planes. It was Bich Lien! She was carrying a stuffed orange kangaroo that belonged to Anthony. What joy! She handed Jim the kangaroo then boarded a plane to Wake Island. Jim thought she was on her way to Guam. We lost track of her.

Jim flew to Guam and then on to California. Anthony and I went to Israel to be with my parents for a short visit. A few weeks later, Jim met my plane in Washington, D.C., and we flew to Albuquerque. On the way, he told me another incredible story.

As he was entering Camp Pendelton (California) refugee camp, Bich Lien suddenly came running across the parking lot shouting, "Ong Jim, Ong Jim!" (Mr. Jim) More joy! He found a family in Albuquerque near his folks who would serve as her sponsor.

The very next day, we met the plane that brought Bich Lien from California to New Mexico. Oh, my thrill of seeing her again! I translated for her as she testified of God's faithfulness to television reporters who covered her story.

But still, that is not the end. Jim and I went to California for a little while to work with refugees. Bich Lien found out that a friend from Vietnam was in the camp. She sent word for him to contact Jim. Jim was able to get a sponsor for Cau from the same church in Albuquerque that had provided Bich Lien's sponsor. Now, Bich Lien and Cau fell in love American style! When we returned a month later, they were making plans for a wedding. Bich Lien had "wanted to marry him in Vietnam but things just didn't work out."

Our final night in Albuquerque, Jim married Bich Lien and Cau. What a celebration and what an ending to the Vietnam chapter of our lives. We left the next day for language study in France . . . but that's another story.

6

Bus Fare

Karen Russey Gross

"In my life in union with the Lord, it is a great joy to me, that . . .
you had the chance of showing that you care for me"
(Phil. 4:10 TEV).

Just a few days before I left Vietnam, I went to the market in the center of Da Lat. I selected bowls and other mementos to take home with me. With two years of bargaining to my credit, I began to bargain. The woman haggled back and forth with me for a few minutes until we settled on a price; but, when I opened my wallet to pay her, I didn't have enough money!

I dug through every corner of my wallet and my pockets. I placed all the money in my possession on the counter and said, "That's all I have."

The woman kindly agreed to accept that amount as full payment for the items I wanted. She carefully wrapped my new treasures in old newspapers and handed them to me. Then she gave me 20 piasters (Vietnamese currency). I didn't understand and tried to give the coins back to her. No, she insisted, I should keep the money for bus fare.

In the two years that I lived in Vietnam, I saw many sad and tragic events. Every night I heard gunfire. I was robbed, frightened, and sometimes insulted, but I *choose* to remember the *real* people of Vietnam as I do that woman in the market: people with many needs and desires, people from a culture very different from mine, but ultimately they were people of grace and kindness.

7

Death and Resurrection

Betty J. Merrell

"Where, Death, is your victory? Where, Death, is your power to hurt?"
(1 Cor. 15:55 TEV).

Spring 1966, outside Da Nang, South Vietnam. I was washing clothes in the wringer washer when the helicopter overhead announced over loudspeakers that all Americans should report to the Hotel Da Nang as soon as possible. We were new in town and not unpacked yet. We had no car and no phone. While I was packing luggage, a chaplain pulled into the yard in a jeep. Lewis Myers, another missionary in town, had already put our names on the list of Americans in Da Nang.

Not too many minutes later, the US officials' instructions gave no hint as to the place we were going or how long we might be gone. US Marines had lined our path from the hotel out to the helicopter lift site. The rifles at their sides sobered our exodus. American military helicopters were scurrying back and forth with passengers and their limited baggage. More than 200 American civilians, including four missionary families, settled into the two wings and a few rooms of the uncompleted Navy hospital about ten miles out of Da Nang. Surrounded by acres of sand on all sides, the hospital was our assigned home for the duration of anticipated battles between government forces and Buddhist "rebels" in Da Nang's streets. On Tuesday after our arrival at our secluded place of refuge, the Red Cross representative came to tell me, "Your dad has died, and has been buried. I am sorry." I had received a letter telling me Dad was sick, and had asked her to find out any news.

The next Sunday was Easter. We joined ambulatory patients and other evacuees packing the new little chapel for Easter morning services. I prayed, "Thank You, Father, for the unexpected comfort I have experienced this week from You, and from all these strangers here." I went on to petition His presence for my mother, my sister, and my brother who were by now in their solitary grieving and grappling 10,000 miles away.

The text and melody of "Christ the Lord Is Risen Today" soared out the open windows to the cloudless skies. "Where, O Death, is now thy sting?" the worshipers questioned in harmony. I listened in quiet awe of it all. Who had removed my sting of death that week? From whence came my peace—and yes, even joy? My dad and I had always been pals. I was in the seventh grade when my mother assigned me to prepare his breakfast and lunch and iron his shirts. He had gently and patiently taught me how to do these tasks. At age 16, one of my favorite ventures was pie and coffee with my dad at the Silver Castle in West Tulsa.

Now, most of the Americans around me were not "religious," at least not visibly so. Their expressions of solace were genuine, but not godly. Our missionary colleagues had poured into me the abundance of God's love and comfort they possessed, but I had more than that.

By stanza four I caught up with my fellow countrymen and women.

Soar we now where Christ has led,
Foll'wing our exalted Head,
Made like him, like him we rise,
Ours the cross, the grave, the skies,
Alleluia!

Of course, of course. "Made like him, like him we rise." His own may indeed rise from the valley of the grave and soar to the skies. The strength of that week and the truths of that moment carried me along the waves of grief. In my soul, I knew that every slight lift was birthed and borne on the wings of prayers raised in my behalf on both sides of the Pacific.

8

House Hunt

Priscilla Compher

"Don't worry about anything, but in all your prayers ask God for
what you need, always asking him with a thankful heart"
(Phil. 4:6 TEV).

We returned to Vietnam in May 1969, physically refreshed and emotionally
restored from our first furlough spent in the US. Our call to missions had been
reaffirmed as we had shared with scores of churches, small and large.
Spiritually we were renewed. We drank in with gratitude the care so lovingly
heaped upon us during our furlough year. We had replenished our personal
clothing and stock of hygiene necessities. We could draw on our supply for
the next four years.

Our request to begin a new ministry in a province where none from our
Mission had lived or worked as yet had been approved. We were full of hope.
We were also anxious as we began to anticipate God's plan for His witness in
Binh Dinh Province.

Our first task was to locate a house for our family of five and to move from
the guest housing unit in Saigon to a place in the city of Qui Nhon. The move
from Saigon to Binh Dinh Province was a distance of approximately 350 miles.

The Lord provided a contact person in Qui Nhon through a missionary
family living in Da Nang. They knew a major in the South Vietnamese army
whose wife and children lived in Qui Nhon.

Bob flew to Qui Nhon with another missionary. They followed up on the
leads provided by the major's wife. We were initiated to something of what life
could be in our new home as a rider on a motorcycle quickly reached under
Bob's watchband to steal his watch.

A lot of Qui Nhon had been destroyed after World War II by the French
military. Likewise, the destruction of government buildings during the Tet
offensive of 1968 was still very evident in the city. After several days, the two
men returned to Saigon. They located a small storefront building on one of the

two main commercial streets of Qui Nhon that would make an ideal place for an activity center program. Bob felt that the area that had housed the now-destroyed government communication facilities would be an ideal location for a church; but the city lacked single-dwelling bungalow houses due to the destruction.

A few days later, Bob and I flew back to Qui Nhon together. We finally decided we would just live in the storefront facility, and headed for the small airport to await our return trip to Saigon.

Minutes before boarding the small DC-3, the major's wife ran up to us, shouting, "Don't leave; stay another day; I have found you a house." We followed her out of the airport to share her find of a larger row house located among other row houses on a sandy street.

Relatives of the owner lived downstairs. A company that provided entertainment for American military installations rented the upstairs. According to the owner, "they dump their garbage out the windows to the street" and "the people often run around barely dressed." If we would rent, she would force them out so we could move in, she urged. We saw possibilities with this house, so we agreed to rent. Even though the house would need much repair and cleaning, we joyfully returned to Saigon to share how the Lord had provided a place for our family.

Interior Decorating

Priscilla Compher

"But if anyone does not take care of his relatives, especially the members of his own family, he has denied the faith and is worse than an unbeliever" (1 Tim. 5:8 TEV).

We were living in Nha Trang after completing language study in Da Lat. We had rented a small three-bedroom bungalow with a bathroom and a room out back, separate from the main house. We planned to turn this back room into our kitchen. My husband built cabinets and counters from our furniture packing crates. He covered the counter tops with roofing tin. Since the room only had a roof with no ceiling, he screened the top of the room with wire material to keep out the rats. He plumbed the room, bringing in water from the well, and we bought a concrete sink. We had a first-class kitchen for our little house.

Missionaries in Vietnam chose to live in housing among the people. Renting a home took on different flavors of difficulties depending on the proposed city of residence.

10

Learning at the Feet of My Sisters

Betty J. Merrell

"Happy are the pure in heart; they will see God!"
(Matt. 5:8 TEV).

I learned so much from my sister missionaries. I basked under the canopies of
their varying faith expressions as they walked before the Lord in the land of
the living (Psalm 116:9): Pauline Routh's quiet and sweet spirit; Dottie Hayes's
kitchen; Celia Moore's elegance; Audrey Roberson's tears; Prissy Tunnell's zest
and zeal; Olive Allen's way without words in the winter years of her life; and
Priscilla Compher's perseverance, to mention but a few.

Three of them taught me four lessons they didn't know they taught. I am
sure they do not remember them, but I do, and I added them to the principles
I live by.

Lesson One. Toni Myers and I stood at the I Corps Army Chapel on a week-
day morning in Da Nang. The wind carried the sometimes odorous smell of
the river to our nostrils that hot morning. "Lordy, that smell is horrible," I
mumbled to Toni. "Yeah, but the breeze feels good, doesn't it? I guess if we
want the breeze, we'll have to take what it brings with it." Woop! I needed that
lesson on the companion rides of good and bad.

Lesson Two started and ended with Toni's next sentence. "And you know,
it's the little things that get to us, isn't it? Like the smell of the river today. Not
the mortars and rockets. We prepare for those and ask God's help. But the irri-
tants—they can get bigger and bigger until . . ." Her voice trailed off in
thought. It was enough. I heard. I now live by that principle on mountains and
molehills.

Lesson Three. The missionary women sat in a room together asking and
answering questions. It was annual retreat time. I was starting to teach my
children at home. I explained my concern that my kindergartener, Dan, often
wanted to sit on my lap during a story lesson. In my newness, I felt I should
keep my teacher role separate from my parent role, so I kept insisting he sit at

his *desk* for lessons just as he would in a formal schoolroom. Veteran missionary Marian Longbottom (five children, and a decade of on-field service beyond mine) smiled at me and said, "What difference does it really make where he sits? Just turn your thoughts to what you're teaching. The other will work out. Besides, we all need some extra closeness at times."

I caught the "lighten-up" message and it has worked forever after.

Lesson Four. Ida Davis didn't seem to talk much—or maybe I just didn't know her well. She was busy with five snazzy, beautiful daughters and the quiet work she usually did behind the scenes.

Now, some of their daughters had been left in the States to go to school. "Ida, how are you doing these days?" I asked. She knew I meant the girls' absence. "Fine," she answered as she always did and with her usual smile. Then, suddenly, those crystal blue eyes fixed on me, and she added, "Betty, in the Christian walk, it just seems like everything would be great all the time, doesn't it? But you know, sometimes it isn't, is it? Sometimes it's hell we deal with." Now, when Ida Davis used *hell*, it was in the context of the faith. But the day she used it in relation to the season of life she was walking through, I saw the raw insides of a woman. I discovered that those on our pedestals are just like the rest of us. We all meet our heavens and hells on the Journey. I like the way Ida did it. She was both real and pure that day.

11

Neighboring

Priscilla Compher

"People learn from one another, just as iron sharpens iron"
(Prov. 27:17 TEV).

Our neighbors in Nha Trang were Vietnamese. Our windows lacked glass panes. Glass blocked the air from getting in, and they enticed boys to throw rocks. But glassless panes also taught us a lot about the activities of our neighbors. Of course, they could easily hear us too. Though our neighbors for the most part were moral, upright citizens, the house across the sandy street was a house of prostitution. We did not explain to our children about the activities in that house. They learned about these from the Vietnamese children. The children told them that the girls living there were *bad* and should be avoided. They used the names with which they labeled the residents. Unfortunately for us, our sons called out these names to the girls one day. The next morning, the windows of our Volkswagen van had been knocked out with rocks.

Our family owned a large, part-German Shepherd dog. He was old, quiet, and gentle most of the time. Being the smart dog he was, he learned to open the gate of our fenced-in yard. On one occasion he chased a boy throwing rocks at him and bit the boy on the leg. Another day he headed toward some women cooking outside their houses over a low, charcoal pot overhanging a small cluster of charcoal. Our dog strolled in the yard unnoticed. At a strategic moment, he grabbed a large hunk of beef being prepared for cooking and headed back to our yard for his feast. Close on his canine heels came the owner of the beef, yelling her *beef* for everyone to hear. Unaware of all that was going on, we heard the commotion and hurried outside. There sat our sanguine friend eating the meat. Over and over again we apologized and offered to pay for the cost of the meat. The victim took the money, but as she left, she walked over to the thief, retrieved the meat from his mouth, turned toward us and said, "There is no time to go to the market to buy more." We tried to be good neighbors. Most of the time we succeeded.

53

12

New Ways for New Days

Priscilla Compher

"Teach them to your children. Repeat them when you are at home and when you are away, when you are resting and when you are working" (Deut. 6:7 TEV).

In the days before homeschooling was popular, I became the first grade teacher for our highly energetic twin boys. They learned to read either sitting in their children's rocking chairs, rocking backward and forward lickity-split, or lying on the floor kicking their legs in the air. I can't explain it, but they became excellent readers. The teachers at the US school (while we were home on our first furlough) were amazed at their "most expressive reading."

I have often been curious. Would they have become such good readers in a normal US classroom situation with 30 or more other six-year-old children?

School for our children happened in a string of settings. Sometimes through the home-school room using the Calvert System; sometimes in boarding schools at Da Lat; in Taiwan; in an international school in Bangkok or Singapore, while living in a missionary-hosted hostel for MKs (missionaries' kids). Occasionally, older MKs would remain in the US for later grades of high school, usually staying with family members. Several times, the teacher for the home school was a two-year missionary whose assignment was to teach MKs.

13

Recreation or Re-creation?

Priscilla Compher

"Homes are built on the foundation of wisdom and understanding. Where there is knowledge, the rooms are furnished with valuable, beautiful things" (Prov. 24:3-4 TEV).

Our children usually finished home-school studies by 12:00 NOON. During the last year of our second term, we usually would finish by 10:00 A.M. So we were constantly in search of wonderful things to do after school hours, and they had to mesh with all other schedules in the household.

Kathy didn't take much of my mental energy in that area. She had several close Vietnamese friends next door and down the street. At our house, they played house or dolls; at their houses, they improvised toys with whatever was around. Kathy wore the *pajama sets* that girls and women in Vietnam wore for everyday (the casual two-piece prints—short or long—now so popular in the US). They ate and slept at each other's houses. At the Comphers, they slept on a bed. At their houses, they slept on mats on the floor. All of the above was recreation for Kathy.

Now the twin boys—well, that was a bigger challenge. We had hoped they could join the Vietnamese boys at play in the schoolyard that extended to our sandy street. The caretaker at the school did not want additional children to look after, so he would chase them out. One evening, Douglas and David saw boys breaking in and stealing from the classrooms. They ran to the caretaker's house to report it. After that, he showed them some appreciation.

American chaplains in our province informed us about swimming pools at several military installations. They introduced us to the commanders, but every six months new commanders came on, and we never knew whether we would be welcomed by the new commander. Some commanders gave permission for us to bring the children. At times a new commander would declare that he wanted the pool used only by the soldiers. We tried to know several places that had pools so something would be available.

The USO Club in Qui Nhon was located on the major air force base near our house. Our boys could ride their bikes through the back entrance, around the airfield, and entertain themselves playing table tennis and pool. At nine or ten years of age they could beat most of the soldiers in both sports. They played three or four times a week until the club closed.

Bob taught Douglas and David to play tennis. For a short period of time they participated in a Vietnamese-style karate class.

A mission board administrator visited most of the missionaries in Vietnam one year. When he returned to Richmond, he recommended that missionaries working in Vietnam be given a vacation outside the country once each year, and that a vacation allowance sufficient to cover travel be provided. What a blessing! We began looking forward to this annual getaway. We chose Singapore and Malaysia for our R-and-R.

We expanded our celebrations of American holidays to include the neighborhood children. On Halloween we bobbed for whatever fruit was available. At birthday parties we taught them American games. In return, they taught our children to celebrate Vietnamese holidays. Our kids marched with the lighted torches, popped firecrackers, and ate moon cakes and special candies during the Oriental New Year festivities. They collected their red envelopes containing gifts of money right alongside their young Vietnamese comrades. They learned to play the local board games.

Twice each year, all the missionaries' children looked forward to playing together at our annual mission retreat, usually around Thanksgiving, and our annual planning meeting in the summer. We traveled to Nha Trang, Saigon, Cam Ranh, Da Lat . . . whatever city was scheduled to host the meeting. Memories were made of this.

Fun and play are a vital slice of life for all young. They provide zest for life and rest from life, both so needed for balance. For missionaries' kids, it is the same. In Vietnam's war environment, the need for balance intensified. Whatever situations we lived and worked in, we could not ignore fun and play for our children and with our children. Indeed, we worked at enriching it for the sake of our children's wholesomeness. With the poverty and temporariness of life in Vietnam, entertainment for children was not a major market of the economy. It was not a market at all. When we were at our best as mothers and fathers in Vietnam, we approached recreation as re-creation.

14

Schoolteachers

Priscilla Compher

"Being wise is better than being strong; yes, knowledge is
more important than strength"
(Prov. 24:5 TEV).

Our twins, Douglas and David, made their professions of faith in Jesus Christ
in the US while on furlough. They studied piano, played on the baseball
team, managed good grades, and participated in most church programs for
their ages. Kathy attended nursery school and participated in a tap and bal-
let class for four-year-olds. All three had made friends easily in their new
home for one year.

When we returned to South Vietnam for our second term, we felt keenly the
responsibility to help them continue to develop educationally, emotionally,
socially, and spiritually, albeit minus the benefit of the schools, churches, and
community programs that had been at their disposal for one year.

For their basic education we used the Calvert home study program from
Baltimore, Maryland, a program rich in the language arts, geography, and history, Western and US. We enjoyed going through the studies from kindergarten to sixth grade during the four years of our second term.

One course we never had to teach was the arithmetic lesson. Vietnamese
schools taught mathematical concepts much earlier than most American
schools. The neighborhood children taught Douglas and David mathematical
knowledge beyond their Calvert grade levels.

Neither Bob nor I were well-trained in science. I felt the homeschool
course was rather weak in science also. So we were grateful for a young
woman assigned to work with us in Qui Nhon the last year of our second four-
year term. Science was her specialty! She supplemented the Calvert science
program for that year. I had been a recipient of God's provision so often in
Vietnam. Every time, I drank in the wonder of it all over again.

15

Stranger on the Beach

Betty J. Merrell

"But have reverence for Christ in your hearts, and honor him as Lord.
Be ready at all times to answer anyone who asks you to explain
the hope you have in you"
(1 Peter 3:15 TEV).

One day, Toni Myers and I took our children to one of the nearby beaches running along the South China Sea that hugged the coastline of our city of Da Nang. The stretch we chose lay in a more protected area since it neighbored a strip reserved for US military personnel. Not too far on the other side, however, we watched a few Vietnamese swimmers sport with the soft white crests of the clear blue sea and laugh with each other in a splashing contest.

The calm and peaceful site banked the mountains behind that loomed up and over as our private giant protectors. After just a few years of peeping in on a string of South Vietnam's beauty spots, I had predicted, "Someday, visionary entrepreneurs are going to discover this beautiful country and turn it into one of the dreams tourists seek and embrace when found. Lush virgin jungles, rivers, mountains, delta, white sands, sloping quiet rolling hills, blue waters, and the eternal lure of Asia are God's rich gifts to a people otherwise poor."

Life in Da Nang since our arrival had served us plate after plate of harried and hurried coping challenges. This unusual getaway afternoon was like a tea party set in the middle of it all—just for our pleasure—a respite of sorts. Though we knew it would be but a momentary diversion, we welcomed such a moment and hurried to accept its invitation. Our families were good at finding reasons for a celebration and at finding ways to provide one. When life cornered us into its pens of poverty and pain, we learned to spot in a jiffy a place or reason to kick up our heels (or lie beside the still waters) and play a bit. And, more often than not, joy was as close as our fingernails.

As we sat there, drinking in the silence broken only by the lap of the azure waters against the white sand in their daily tryst, and the carefree play sounds of our six children, Michael, Laura, Margaret, Dan, Tim, and Grey, another figure came in sight. We watched as he came closer. American, it seemed—one could never be sure in the blurring mosaic of faces of the world in Vietnam. When he spoke, we knew he was American. "I'm not believing this," he said. "Are you Americans—wives and children—*here*?" "Yes," we affirmed, "we are." We grinned. "I didn't know any American families were still in Vietnam. I thought all had been sent home." "Well, not us, huh? Here we are." We sort of teased him along toward the question we anticipated. "Well, why in tarnation are you here? I wouldn't bring my wife and children here for nothing!" "Nor would we," I answered. "We wouldn't come 'for nothing' either. We came to South Vietnam for *something*! A big something, really." I paused for his next question. "Now, what could that be?" There it was. The question. We shared lightly, not with labor or length, our sensed call from God as reason for coming to South Vietnam and for still being here at that time.

In a moment, he walked on, shaking his head. He couldn't fathom it; he couldn't buy it. He walked out of our lives in the same manner as he had walked in—except perhaps with a new subject for thought.

In Vietnam, many Vietnamese people asked the stranger's question. Recently, a young mechanic was putting a belt on the alternator of my car in Birmingham. He was small of stature, Asian. He could be Vietnamese. I hesitated, then ventured, "Excuse me, sir, are you Vietnamese?" "No, Thai," he answered proudly. I told him of my visits to Thailand; that led into telling him of our time spent in South Vietnam.

After a while, he looked at me quizzically and asked the stranger on the beach's question, "Why you go to Vietnam?" I thought once again. What words should I choose to use in this brief moment I have with yet another stranger. "We believed God sent us to South Vietnam," I said slowly, looking straight into his black eyes. "Can you accept that?" I smiled. He shrugged his diminutive shoulders and grinned back. "OK by me!" he answered. And we became friends in that moment.

16

Street Sounds

Dottie Hayes

"The master . . . said to his servant, 'Hurry out to the streets and alleys of
the town, . . . Go out to the country roads and lanes'"
(Luke 14:21-23 TEV).

After some weeks in our first neighborhood in Saigon, we began to notice the
many street sounds of people selling their wares. Tim began to notice someone calling out something that sounded like "ti-mo-thy" to him. Each time we
would hear it, Tim would say, "He's calling me again." One day Tim decided
he would check this out. He found a little man selling iced sugar-cane juice.
We later learned that he was saying "Mia Glacie."

Hope soon picked up several sounds and mimicked them in the house to
the delight of her big brother. One of these was *banh bò*. She would put a basket, or anything she could find, on her head and yell *"banh bò"* imitating the
Vietnamese woman who sold these delightful little sweets. The *banh bò* was
stacked in a flat basket which she carried on her head.

One Sunday during the worship service at the English-speaking church in
Saigon, Hope put a song book on top of her head and began to shout, *"banh
bò, banh bò."* Everyone seated around us got very tickled but the boys enjoyed
it the most. What a sister!

We continued through the years to learn the new sounds and discover the
many delightful new tastes found on the streets of Vietnam.

17

Surprise at 45

Audrey Roberson

"'My thoughts,' says the Lord, 'are not like yours, and my
ways are different from yours'"
(Isa. 55:8 TEV).

With our first furlough over, we returned to our evangelistic work in the mountain city of Da Lat, where our Mission operated a language school for its new
missionaries. Bill was also responsible for the operation of the language school
and we were grateful for several new, young missionary families as students.

By the year 1965, the war was heating up considerably as compared with
the time of our entry in 1960. Ample evidence in Da Lat told us that a war was
going on. Many American military planes flew low over our house, landing
and taking off from the small military airport only two or three miles away.
Dreaded cannons were often heard in the distance.

Our three children were in school. I had taught them for two years during
our previous term at Nha Trang. But the time had come that Hanes, our oldest child, should begin his studies in the eighth grade in Bangkok, Thailand.
Sending him off was one of our most painful experiences. Our two daughters,
Amelia and Nancy, were in the sixth and fourth grades in the Christian and
Missionary Alliance School in Da Lat. So, I could give time to continuing language study, as well as helping Bill more in his work.

By late fall, I began to feel sickly. I found it difficult to keep up with my
schedule. I imagined everything that could be wrong with me, including cancer. More than a month passed before I decided to seek the advice of a medical
doctor. I was 44; I wanted the counsel of the best doctor I could locate. After
discussing the matter with several persons, I decided I should go to Dr. De, a
World Health doctor, who ran a clinic in Saigon.

To prepare for the visit, I wired Dottie Hayes, a missionary in Saigon, that
I was coming. I asked her to make an appointment for me and also asked to
stay with them, if it was convenient.

Making the flight to Saigon was no easy trip even when well. I recall the plane sat on the ground at the Tan Son Nhut airport for 40 minutes waiting for military flights that always held the right of way. No one met me at the Saigon airport.

Our plane arrived during the long Asian noon-break when the city completely stopped its work to rest. This included most taxis, of course. An American man trying to get downtown offered to let me go in the taxi he was taking. Weary and hot, I traveled with a complete stranger, thinking little about it at the time.

I was not sure of Dottie's address, but I was certain I could find her house when I reached that area of the city. I asked the taxi driver to let me out at a point along the way and thanked the American man. With my suitcase and a smelly box of fresh strawberries in hand, I walked four or five blocks in the midday heat to find their house.

Realizing everyone was probably resting, I rang their gate bell. I waited. Nothing happened. I rang again, and still no response. Finally, I called out through the gate, "Dottie . . . Dottie," in my very pronounced southern drawl. By that time, it dawned on me that the electricity was off, as was often the case. The bell wasn't working. Inside, my voice drifted in from the street. Dottie said to Herman, "That sounds like Audrey, but it just couldn't be." She looked out at the front gate to see if anyone was there. Sure enough, there I stood, and she came running.

Dottie alternated expressing her delight in seeing me with her surprise that I was in Saigon. Then I learned she had not received my telegram—which also explained why no one met me at the airport.

We got to work immediately making arrangements to see the doctor. Meanwhile, in Da Lat, Bill and the family anxiously awaited word. I saw the doctor and after waiting several hours he announced that I was expecting a baby!

The only way I could get the news to Bill and the two children at home was to send a telegram, with no assurance that it would be delivered.

When the wire arrived in Da Lat, Bill was perplexed with its meaning, for it only read, "FOURTH DUE IN JULY (Stop)." Finally, it hit. The news was gladly and immediately spread to all other missionaries, friends, and our son in Bangkok.

The war escalated rapidly. We moved to Saigon and the area where we discovered new trials and difficulties each day. To add to our troubles, Dr. De fled the country before the baby arrived, leaving me with a stranger to deliver the baby. But you know what? John William arrived safely on the evening of July 26, the very day on which my mother had delivered her last boy when she was also 45. What an ending! And what a beginning! John has blessed our family in special ways across the subsequent years of missionary service and retirement.

18

The Divine Presence

Mary Humphries

"The Lord is with me, I will not be afraid; what can anyone do to me?"
(Psalm 118:6 TEV).

Finding adequate medical care for our children was a major concern of every missionary parent in Vietnam. Somehow God always provided. We had been in Saigon less than one week when Tracy, our eight-month-old baby daughter, became very ill with a high fever. The only available physician was a Frenchman who did not speak English, and we could not speak French. Instructions on the label of the prescription bottle were written in French. I'm not sure what we did about that; I imagine we made the first of many guesses.

For two or three days, I sponged Tracy's feverish infant body and I held her during periods of fretful sleep. As I rocked, I prayed for God's healing. I also found myself asking, "Lord, why did you call us to this place? Do you know how helpless I feel with this sick baby?"

The virus, or whatever was causing the fever, soon ran its course. Tracy was back to normal in a few days. I was taking baby steps in learning to depend on the Lord in a far-off place.

When Tracy was two, she fell from a ledge outside the second floor of our house. Tracy was always a climber, and she followed her two brothers everywhere. A fall was inevitable. The young Vietnamese girl who worked for us was nearby when Tracy fell and immediately picked her up. She ran to us with the still, limp body, beginning to turn blue, in her arms. I grabbed her, Jim and I ran to the car, and the minute I slammed the door Tracy began to cry. We rushed to the nearby Third Field Army hospital, and the army doctors on duty gave her their full attention until they were certain she had no serious injuries.

When we returned home, we walked to the spot where Tracy had fallen. Square cement stepping-stones were scattered all about the yard, but she had landed on soft ground less than two inches from one of the stones. We gave thanks to God for His watchcare and protection. Our faith grew that day.

Our oldest son, Matt, cut his face across his cheekbone as he collided with a large ceramic flower pot while running through the churchyard one Sunday night. Jim grabbed him up immediately and ran to a jeep where the driver had the engine running to take him to Third Field Army hospital. Jim threw his Bible on the seat. I sat beside Matt in the emergency room as he lay on the metal table with a sheet covering his face except for a round hole which exposed the large open gash. I watched young Dr. Hayes, not a plastic surgeon, not even a surgeon but a family practice specialist, sew up Matt's face. I could see the cheekbone beneath the open skin. The doctor skillfully placed about 65 stitches in three layers of skin. I believe a plastic surgeon could not have done better, for today there is hardly a trace of a scar. Surely that doctor's hand had divine guidance as he made every stitch.

Jim left me at the hospital with Matt that night and returned to the church to preach. When he opened his Bible, he saw Matt's blood in a line across the gilded edges of its pages, all the way from Genesis to Revelation. As he looked at the blood line of his own son on the pages of the Bible, he told the story and then reminded the congregation of the blood of God's Son which was shed for them, and "*that* blood line runs throughout the Bible from Genesis to Revelation," he said with new emotions. The son's blood on the pages of Jim's Bible had imprinted an intense new understanding of how God felt about the Son's blood on the pages of Jim's Bible.

19

The Fire

Betty J. Merrell

"God will put his angels in charge of you to protect you wherever you go" (Psalm 91:11 TEV).

Fall 1964, Da Lat, South Vietnam. A coastal typhoon pushed cold winds and torrential rains up to Da Lat, a resort town nestled in the mountains. Da Lat was ideal for our concentrated study of the Vietnamese language.

A small portable kerosene heater spread little heat in the big old French-style house we had rented. We were cold, and the clothes hanging on the portable rack were as wet as when they were hung there a day ago.

We decided to try a fire in the fireplace. The heat warmed us some, and the clothes began drying. I tucked our sons, Dan and Tim (ages four and two), in their bunk beds in an upstairs bedroom. I covered them with quilts that lovingly had been put together by a grandmother. When the fire in the fireplace was down to the smoldering ashes, I went to bed. A bathroom separated the boys' bedroom and ours.

At 2:00 A.M. I awoke. An eerie, bright light scampered along the bathroom floor. I ran to the boys' bedroom. One of Ron's shower slippers, a rubber, thonged sandal, lay burning a few inches from the quilt folds hanging from Tim's lower bunk. Under the slipper was a hole, burned through from the wildfire raging within the walls downstairs. The fire was looking for more places to go. In the hole it had bored, it found its breath of fresh air, its freedom to break into the upstairs part of the house.

I ran back to shake Ron, then scurried the drowsy boys outside. Ron and the next-door neighbor, our language teacher, went for help. While they were gone, I pondered, *Who awakened me, heavy sleeper that I am?* In just a few more minutes, flames would have grabbed Tim's quilt and held him captive. His terrified screams would have awakened me.

Before long I felt a presence by our chosen refuge slot. I looked up and Mrs. Thanh, our language teacher's wife from next door, stood by me. We couldn't communicate in words. I had only been in Vietnam three months. She would smile comfort and I would smile my gratitude. Every little bit, she would walk over and pat me on the shoulder. I uttered the only Vietnamese words appropriate to my vocabulary, her understanding, and the circumstances: *Cam on, Cam on* (Thank you, Thank you).

If you should ask me about this night, I emphatically would tell you, there was an angel inside the house when the fire started, and there was an angel outside the house in the orchard where we retreated among the trees.

Fireplaces in Da Lat were not usually built for fires. They were made of mortar mixed with much sand and a little cement. The overheated sand turned into flame as it encountered wood. "The fireplace is for charcoal pots," a veteran missionary in Vietnam explained to the Merrells—after the fire.

20

The Letter Box

Marian Longbottom

"Write down for the coming generation what the Lord has done,
so that people not yet born will praise him"
(Psalm 102:18 TEV).

My mother saved all our family's letters to her from 1955-89. I've only gone through several boxes. These excerpts reveal some news and views from our hearth and heart in Vietnam.

Lynda, my daughter, was a senior student at Morrison Academy in Taiwan when we had to leave Vietnam on April 4, 1975. Tommy, Terry, and I went to Taichung, Taiwan, to await her graduation in May. Danny was finishing his freshman year at Morrison. A few days after our arrival in Taiwan, Lynda asked me, "Mother, do you realize that I probably can never go home again?" I confess I had not yet thought from that perspective. The deep emotions that arose within me in response to her question will never be forgotten.

June 2, 1975. Letter from Lynda (17 years old).
"I'm excited to go to Guam and see all those Vietnamese refugees. I love those people so much! It is hard to believe, still, that we'll never go back home (to Vietnam) because of the situation. I'm going to miss it so much. I already do!"

Date unknown. Letter from me—probably one of those times we were on our way to Bangkok, Thailand—maybe when Sammy first went to the International School of Bangkok as a high school freshman.
"Rachel James gave us an exciting traffic-jam ride to the airport in Saigon. Plane was due to leave at 10:20. We arrived at the airport at 10:15. Ahem! However, just as I ran up to the desk, they were then calling the arrival of the flight from Hong Kong. So, we would make the flight. Said chauffeur Rachel,

'Well, the Lord didn't do anything about the Bangkok street traffic, but the plane in the air traffic ways was late. So!'"

It seems like we always returned from out-of-country trips with some strange things in our luggage, or even worse, hand-carried. Would you believe we brought things like three plastic toilet seats?

August 6, 1968. Letter from me written during flight from Singapore to Saigon after a vacation.

"Stopped at a supermarket on the way to the Bangkok airport this morning. I bought treasures like a couple of cans of furniture polish, some hand lotion, and rubber gloves! As always, I've ended up with a packload of stuff not ordinarily found in a woman's purse."

July 1, 1968. Letter from me—from Da Lat.

"Jimmy has been working on getting his bulletin board made and put up. Now he wants me to help him find some good stuff to put on it—ha! He thinks that Sammy has already gotten all the 'good stuff.'"

August 16, 1968. Letter from me—from Da Lat.

"The Bengs family, our family, and one summer missionary flew to Da Lat on Saturday morning. It was just past noon when we got into town. Came into a musty, damp house, cold, no water—all hungry and tired. Managed to put together a snack before very long and then to fix a spaghetti dinner.

"Sunday was busy with feeding the gang, on to Sunday School, Vietnamese church, and then an English service for our families and one American serviceman.

"Sam was gone most of the afternoon, visiting at Trai Mat, and returning back to show a film at Chi Lang. (These are villages outside Da Lat.)

"Seemed like we would just finish washing dishes (15 people use a whole lot of dishes!) and it was time to start preparing another meal. Ever since coming home I have fed 15-18 people each meal. On Monday the two summer missionaries who worked in Da Nang came. Tuesday morning Miss Aliene Johnson (74 years old) came by helicopter from Cam Ranh. She's staying with us temporarily for two months. The earlier part of the week seemed like Christmas because we had people sleeping all over the house."

September 6, 1968. Following a trip to take Sammy to Bangkok.

"Had a good trip, Bangkok to Saigon. Left for Da Lat the next morning. It was 12:30 when we finally got to our house. The seven journeymen (short-term missionaries) and the Gayles are here. Miss Johnson was busy preparing lunch so got busy immediately. Takes about all my time cooking, 13-15 people each meal. I might add that we still operate the Longbottom Hotel and love doing it!"

June 1973.

"While in Hong Kong for a few days vacation following Jim's graduation from Morrison Academy in Taiwan, Danny became ill with shingles in the eye. Sam, Lynda, and a guest returned to Vietnam the day Danny entered the hospital. Because the two youngest boys were on my passport, Jimmy had to stay in Hong Kong and work out the processes for getting a passport for himself and Danny and a visa for Vietnam before they could travel. That is another whole story of praise to the Lord.

"Danny was in the hospital for three weeks. We were faced with the possibility of his losing sight in one eye. It is so wonderful to know God and be His child. During these past few weeks I have claimed many of His promises over and over. His strength has carried us through these experiences. When we knew Danny might lose all of his sight in the one affected eye, or learned of the suspicion of a more serious underlying something, perhaps leukemia, it was God's grace and strength which gave us confidence. Whatever the outcome, we knew that God was with us, and His grace is sufficient to *any* need. Truth!

"Is it any wonder that over and over I say, 'Thank You, Lord' when the blood tests all turned out normal, when Danny responded so quickly to the doctor's treatment? How good it has been this week to see Danny's right eye opened normally wide most of the time and know that his vision is OK. What a blessing! What a blessing, indeed!

"The last examination by the doctor showed no damage and all was pronounced clear. How marvelous to hear the doctor say that we could return home to Vietnam after a one-month separation from the rest of the family. We feel like we're sitting on top of the world right now and it's great! God is so good!"

21

The Missionary Is a Mom

Priscilla Compher

"I am always aware of the Lord's presence; he is near,
and nothing can shake me"
(Psalm 16:8 TEV).

December 1963, Richmond, Virginia. I am six months pregnant with our third child. Bob and I sit around the conference table with the trustees of the Foreign Mission Board of the Southern Baptist Convention. We are seeking appointment to serve as missionaries under that Board in Vietnam. Most questions are directed to my husband.

Eyeing me directly, a member says he has a question for me. "Do you feel comfortable taking your children into a war-torn country?"

I sit there . . . 27 years old, thinking. I remember God's call to foreign missions as a GA, 13 years old.* I've now worked my way through college, married a missions volunteer, and taught school to help him finish seminary. He has served as pastor of a church in Virginia. I sit here sensing the presence of God throughout all these stages of my life. Now, I'm ready to answer the question. "I believe the Lord will be with us and will give us the wisdom and the strength as needed."

Soon, we entered South Vietnam to begin our first term as missionaries. That answer soon came alive.

Within several months after reaching Da Lat for language study, our three-year-old twin sons awoke one morning with low-grade fevers. That morning they could not stand, sit, hold up their heads, or use their arms. In fear we wondered what strange, tropical disease had attacked them. Frantically, we ran to ask for advice from another missionary family. They directed us to a missionary physician from another Mission who had come up to Da Lat from Saigon for a few days vacation. He assured us that our sons were suffering from a viral middle ear infection. In three days we should notice recovery, he promised. We knew the Lord had sent this physician to Da Lat to give us the assurance we needed as we faced this first scary time in Vietnam.

During that first year, our baby daughter fell, cutting her head. She needed stitches. One of the twins ran into an open pipe, cutting himself; he needed stitches. The other twin had an allergic reaction to a probable overdose of typhoid serum. When he failed to respond to treatment under a local physician, I begged a ride on an American embassy plane to Nha Trang, to an American military hospital. When I arrived, I begged a ride with an American contract worker to the hospital. At the hospital, I noticed the old, faded blue Volkswagen that belonged to a missionary in Nha Trang. The missionary wife had a dental appointment at the hospital. God knew I needed help that day. All along the way He had arranged assistants to help me.

Emergencies filled our first term. David's foot in a kettle of boiling water, Douglas's finger chopped off at the end and skin grafts that followed, Kathy's drink of rubbing alcohol while running high fever, the twins' allergic reaction to a penicillin shot, my dengue fever, and a miscarriage that led to evacuation by plane to the military hospital at Nha Trang. Of course, we got to experience the usual—and some unusual—kid maladies such as chicken pox, mumps, numerous intestinal flulike viruses, parasites, and head lice.

But through it all, God stayed true to my answer to the trustee that December day in 1963.

GA is the abbreviation for Girls' Auxiliary, a missions education organization in Southern Baptist churches until 1970 when its name changed to Girls in Action.

22
The Refrigerated Van

Priscilla Tunnell

"I have learned to be satisfied with what I have"
(Phil. 4:11b TEV).

"Honey, I'm all for sharing everything I have but this is a little ridiculous—taking the missionary spirit a little too far. Remember the hours of looking, pricing, and comparing we did to pick out just the right one? That single vegetable drawer is what finally sold me on this model. It felt so good to be able to purchase a new refrigerator."

"Are you sure this is the only way to fix the problem? I realize that the bottom of the van is rusted, the battery fell out, and without a battery the van won't run. I also realize that it needs to be fastened in securely. But is using the vegetable drawer from my new refrigerator the best alternative?"

"Well, OK, go ahead. I can put a box in the refrigerator for the vegetables. After all, we can boast of the only refrigerated van in the country."

23
The Real Throne Room

Margaret Gayle

"How we laughed, how we sang for joy!" (Psalm 126:2*a* TEV).

When our family was asked by the Vietnamese Mission to move to Cam Ranh, we had heard about the missionary house and its *interesting* features. Jim and I thought it a delightful place to live, and some of our three sons' fondest memories are of this house.

The wooden-framed house was roofed with tin and floored with cement. The two front bedrooms were walled with large planks lined with screen wire. Cracks between the planks let in some light and provided ventilation against the oppressive heat. Fun was when a mouse also squeezed through the cracks and the boys could watch him play around while they lay on their beds for the traditional afternoon rest.

The original house had been built around a well and that well was a permanent fixture in our small living room. Our family laughed when GIs would visit us and say, "Oh, a real American home!" They were so excited with seeing a family that they missed the unique Smithsonian features.

The most talked-about feature of the Cam Ranh house, though, was the bathroom. Nobody who came to our house missed seeing it. We saw to it. Actually, it wasn't a *bath* room since bathing was done outside in a small shed an American serviceman had graciously rigged for us and furnished with a large water drum complete with pipes and spigot—and I might add, a place where sun-warm water baths could be taken most hours of the day.

Inside the house, though, was this other room, humorously nicknamed by some former missionary resident, the *throne* room. The term *throne* literally depicts the 2½-feet-high platform on which the commode was set. To get to the top, one had to climb several wooden steps. These steps provided our family and our guests with many mighty laughs. No matter how gingerly anyone tried to climb those steps, they were sure to creak loudly, in announcement of someone's ascendency to the throne.

24

He Wired It Together

Priscilla Tunnell

"I have the strength to face all conditions by the power that Christ gives me" (Phil. 4:13 TEV).

Our house was filled with excitement. It was time for Mission meeting and everyone was coming to our town. The arrangements had been made, and on this day Gene and I were to drive the two vans down the mountain to the small airport to pick up a bunch of missionary families who were flying in by airplane. The road down the mountain was steep, narrow, and had sharp curves.

Not far out of town, Gene's van stopped and we discovered a broken belt. Off came my stockings and a belt was made. Good thing I wasn't trying to impress all the old-timers by looking my best!

As we began the winding descent, the clutch on my car went out. After a wild and hair-raising stretch, I managed to butt the van to a stop against an embankment. Out came the tow rope—all six feet of it.

Gene asked, "Do you want to drive the van with the new belt and lead, or take 'the brakeless wonder' and follow?"

My answer was simple and straight to the point, "Neither!"

Gene quickly informed me that neither was not an option. Faced with no alternative, I chose to follow. With my eyes glued to Gene's brake lights, my hands in a death grip on the steering wheel, and my stomach in knots in my throat, I maneuvered my tag-along vehicle down the narrowest, steepest decline I'd ever traveled.

Once at the airport, Gene got some help. He borrowed a coat hanger from someone's garment bag and wired the clutch this time. I crawled in the back to reclaim my nerve and left the drive back up the mountain to someone whose intrepidity remained intact. I was duck soup!

Our Labors

———

1
A Little Child Shall Lead Them

Priscilla Compher

"Even a child shows what he is by what he does"
(Prov. 20:11a TEV).

After language study in the mountain city of Da Lat, we moved to Nha Trang, a coastal city in the central part of the country, joining another missionary family who was leading the work of the existing two small churches. We were asked to develop a new church in the Phuoc Hai area of Nha Trang, a city of over 500,000 people. Phuoc Hai was located on the outskirts of the city. It consisted of one partly paved road, several dirt roads, and scores of tiny sandy alleyways where thousands of families lived in tiny houses built of discarded tin, plywood, cardboard, and occasionally some building blocks of questionable source.

We planned to begin with an activity center, developing programs that would help the families in the community. After our contacts with the people, we chose to begin with adult Bible studies, children's Bible clubs, evangelistic films, and worship services.

No money had been budgeted for this new work and as yet we had no Vietnamese Christian to help us. We prayed for the Lord's guidance and help.

The needed finances came in a mysterious way. An American serviceman stationed at Clark Air Force Base in the Philippines was assigned to a reconnaissance group that flew missions over Vietnam. For these flights he received combat pay. He wanted to use this money for ministry in Vietnam. He learned of our names and work and started mailing us money orders for $600 through the local postal system. (We have never met this man and through the last 20 years have lost touch with him.) Amazingly, every money order reached us in spite of the unreliable postal system that our own families feared to use.

With this money we rented several small rooms, bought equipment and supplies, and printed brochures telling about the program at the activity center in Phuoc Hai.

The Lord did not give us a Vietnamese Christian to help us, however. Instead He chose to use our five-year-old twin boys with bright blue eyes, rosy cheeks, and blond hair. These sights, rare in Phuoc Hai, and their outgoing personalities charmed the people in the area and won friends, even among those who did not readily accept foreigners.

David and Douglas, always ahead of us, ran up and down the alleyways entering family dwellings boldly. In their simple but clear Vietnamese they announced the opening of the center and handed out the brochures.

For the next two years our children served with us and a nucleus of a church developed. Another missionary family came, strengthened this church, and a building was bought.

For our second term of missionary service in Vietnam, we were assigned to the central coastal town of Qui Nhon. We were the first Baptist missionaries assigned to Qui Nhon and the surrounding rural province.

Once again by being the only Western family with children, we became known quickly. Our twins, now vibrant eight-year-olds, and our doll-faced, dark-haired, five-year-old daughter joined in supporting us in the work and in the mistakes we made.

In Qui Nhon we developed an expanded activity center, adding tailoring, English and kindergarten classes, and a lending library. The children helped prepare the books to be checked out. This process not only included cataloging the books, in Vietnam it also included cutting the pages open in each book. Often, printed books were sold uncut. The children helped us bring in their friends for our first children's Bible study classes. They made friends for us as they easily mingled with the Vietnamese people in our different classes and along the sandy road where we lived. And likewise they saved us from danger several times as they learned from their Vietnamese friends that trouble was brewing. They were the red flag bearers who told us when we needed to stay inside for a few days.

David, Douglas, and Kathy not only lived in Vietnam with us, they ministered with us.

When all missionaries left in 1975, five Vietnamese families quietly continued to gather at Phuoc Hai Baptist Church for worship, although the sign for the church was removed. Later, the church moved to invisibility. In 1991, hoping that Baptists would be tolerated by the Communist government, the church again put up a sign identifying themselves as a Baptist church. Shortly afterward, the government officially closed the building and warned the group not to try to worship there again.

After 1975 all the churches in Qui Nhon were closed. Yet groups of Christians remained faithful. Today we receive letters from some of the leaders bearing testimony to their personal faithfulness. We believe that testimonies of our children growing up in Vietnam contributed to their faith in our Lord Jesus Christ.

2

And Death Begets Life

Rosalie Beck

"How wonderful it is to see a messenger coming across the mountains,
bringing good news, the news of peace!"
(Isa. 52:7a TEV).

You would find the city of Da Lat on a picture postcard—shops and market-place propped on a level nook of the mountains; homes nuzzling the valleys. In the 1920s, the French colonialists decided to turn the village into a quiet, beautiful resort center, a place to retreat, and retreat they did. However, they limited the Vietnamese and tribal peoples' travel in their own land.

Those European colonialists created a quiet, lovely city in Vietnam. French-styled homes, streets, water system. Structures built for permanence. The French engineered the damming of a small river to create Ho Xuan Huong, the Lake of the Perfume of Spring. Planners added a road over the top of the dam, and it became the major thoroughfare for traffic to the central market and the bus station.

After the French lost Vietnam, the Vietnamese and tribal peoples moved freely once again to Da Lat. It became a city of some 80,000 persons. Refugees from other parts of the country came to the city they saw as a safe haven. It was said that peaceful Da Lat was the site chosen by both Communists and government forces as an R-and-R center. Fighting began around the city in the early 1960s, but typically, the city lay there mum, watching.

Baptists arrived in Da Lat in the early 1960s. New missionaries spent their first year and more studying at the Vietnam Baptist Language Center placed in the secluded and cool Da Lat hills.

Earl and Sherry Bengs became the first full-time missionaries assigned to Da Lat. When they completed language study, they began to establish churches in the area. I arrived in Da Lat in the spring of 1974 as the station journeyman.

When refugees started fleeing to Da Lat, they settled in valleys that wound their trails through the mountainous terrain. The refugees formed closed societies. Missionaries and Christians in Da Lat found it difficult to establish relationships with residents of these communities. We asked God many times to open the valleys and people there so we could take His hope to them.

One Saturday morning, a loud noise jerked me awake. I thought it was a sonic boom since Vietnamese jets flying over Da Lat often jolted our ears and nerves. I walked to the Bengses' home later in the morning. Sherry was concerned. She had timed the boom about the time that Earl's plane was due to take off for Saigon at the Da Lat airport down the mountain. Before long we learned Earl's plane had taken off safely, but a major tragedy had jarred Da Lat.

A young Vietnamese pilot, assigned to a new jet, decided to fly over his mother's house to let her see his plane. She lived in a refugee community at the base of the dam. As he slowed to fly over her makeshift home, the plane's afterburner shut down. When he tried to restart the engine, his plane blew apart, showering burning jet fuel and debris over the dam-road into the lake. The boom was his exploding craft and maybe the cries of the 58 people swept into the lake. Many bodies were never recovered. Scores of others on their way to or from the market were taken to the Province Hospital for treatment of serious fuel burns.

Nga, one of the fine Vietnamese young people in our church, came to the Bengses' home a short time following the crash. "Several of my school friends were injured and are in the Province Hospital," she reported. She was concerned about their need for better care and asked if we could do anything. Earl called Dr. Gene Griffith at the World Vision Clinic down the mountain in the village of Lien Hiep. Griffith recently had returned to South Vietnam after spending several months studying burn treatment at Seely Hospital in Galveston, Texas. He brought special burn treatment equipment back with him. He agreed to help the students if we could bring them to his clinic.

I rode with Nga and Earl to the hospital to visit her friends. I still cringe at the memory of the dirt, the stench. The Province Hospital was the only medical facility for miles; the small staff was at the point of exhaustion. The large, open rooms were filled with beds, all with the wounded in them. Services were limited to emergency care and major medical attention. One of Nga's friends had just died, his body lay covered by a sheet. We determined to move the others to the World Vision Clinic at Lien Hiep.

Da Lat had no ambulances, so Earl converted the station van into a temporary ambulance. We made several trips down the mountain. I held IV bottles and tried to keep the three or four stretchers from banging around as Earl cautiously maneuvered the twisting road. When we arrived at the hospital, Griffith's staff took the patients into clean rooms where he examined them and started treatment.

We ended up taking more than just students to the World Vision center. A young mother, an older man, others. God opened door after door to minister to the people. Not a single one of Nga's friends taken to Dr. Griffith and his staff died. God's grace flowed over the patients there. We visited regularly. As they began to return to their homes, they invited us to visit them. Earl, Sherry, and I, plus many Da Lat Christians worked with the people as God moved among them.

Nga introduced us to Miss Yen, a professor at Da Lat University, who initiated the opening of doors for our missionaries to train Vietnamese students in social ministries. The students asked, "Why are you doing this for us?" Each time, we'd say, "Because God loves you, and thus, so do we." This care of the community left its mark on the people of Da Lat. Many, previously unreached, became believers, and eternal wholeness wound its way into the valleys filled with refugees.

3

Christian Hope

Rosalie Beck

"Why am I so sad? Why am I so troubled?
I will put my hope in God, and once again I will praise him,
my savior and my God"
(Psalm 42:5 TEV).

Other cultures understand Christian hope in ways different from the average North American Christian. We quote Scripture verses about the *hope of glory* and our *hope in God*. Many Vietnamese believers had a much more concrete understanding of hope. For them, hope was God actively involved in their lives, keeping promises today and tomorrow. I learned the power of this perspective from Ba Son (Mrs. Shung), a member of the church in Da Lat.

The mother of eight children, Ba Son was married to an electrician in the Army of Vietnam; he was not a Christian. She had become a believer after some of her children began attending our church. A quiet and shy woman, she rarely spoke in the service; but she attended as regularly as possible, and she brought her children faithfully.

In the fall of 1974, her husband suffered a charge of more than 60,000 volts of electricity through his body in an accident. The medical personnel were amazed that he did not die immediately, and treated him halfheartedly because they assumed he would die shortly. Ba Son came to missionary Earl Bengs and asked him to witness to her husband and help him receive better care in the military hospital. Her Christian hope-in-action gave her the assurance that her husband would not die until he had a chance to respond to the gospel.

For two months her husband lingered; the medical personnel kept careful watch but could only help with medication for the pain. Earl regularly met with the dying man and checked to make sure he received good care. Ba Son and the church members prayed for the dying man's soul. God fulfilled the promise of hope to Ba Son when her husband became a Christian through Earl's teaching and the church's prayers. When he died, she spoke to the church about how good God was in answering her prayers and saving her husband—her Christian hope transferred to action.

One Sunday morning after the service, Ba Son asked for a moment in which to give testimony to God's goodness. She received a pittance from the government as an army widow; she and several of her older children had to work very hard to make ends meet. She told us how that week she had no money with which to buy food for her children. In despair she went to God, affirming her hope that God would provide. A friend of one of her children gave the child a lottery ticket. The ticket won and Ba Son received enough money to care for her family. I've reflected: Did God use the child's gift as a channel to honor a desperate woman's prayer of hope and faith?

In March 1975, as the nation of Vietnam fell to the Communists, Ba Son and her children made their way to Saigon, where they thought they would be safe. She came to the Vietnam Baptist Mission headquarters in the Gia Dinh section of the city to see missionaries Sherry and Earl Bengs. As chair of the Mission, Earl had to be in Saigon during this time of crisis, and the city of Da Lat, their home, had already fallen to the Communists. Sherry took Ba Son to arrange for some of the family's needs and then dropped her off at her house. As they parted, Sherry told Ba Son that within the next few days she would fly to Singapore and did not know when, or if, she would see her again. The Vietnamese woman wept at the thought of not seeing her friend again. To comfort her, Sherry hugged Ba Son and said, "Well, we know we will see each other when Christ returns." Ba Son's head shot up and she asked, "When will that be?" As Sherry explained this most vital part of the Christian hope, she realized Ba Son had never been taught about the Second Coming. Somehow, Ba Son had missed the ultimate promise to believers of God's victory over evil and of the establishment of the kingdom of God—this ultimate hope.

As Sherry talked, Ba Son's face lightened and she smiled joyfully: "Christ is coming back for me." Even though she did not know when it would occur, Ba Son was convinced immediately of the truth of this hope. She lived her life bathed in the hope of God's children, and she taught me how vital a part of my life that hope should be.

4

For Lack of a Wall

Margaret Gayle

"My children, our love should not be just words and talk;
it must be true love, which shows itself in action"
(1 John 3:18 TEV).

One day this young Vietnamese man in the coastal city of Cam Ranh dropped by our house. He had just recently become a Christian. He asked Jim, my husband, if he would be willing to share about Jesus to his high school friend, and without another word he left. A few days later he returned, bringing his friend, Man Dong, from a tribal Montagnard village about 12 kilometers away. Man Dong listened intently as Jim shared the good news. Then immediately he opened his heart to the Lord.

With some trepidation, Jim presented Man Dong as a candidate for baptism to the church in Cam Ranh. Customarily the Vietnamese people had little to do with tribal people, and Jim was afraid the congregation would refuse to fellowship with Man Dong. But to our joy and amazement, the Vietnamese Christians readily accepted him as a fellow believer.

Some weeks later Man Dong arrived at church with his two brothers and their wives. Soon they too believed, were received by the church, and were baptized. The three brothers faithfully attended church every Sunday. Then one day their elderly father came with his family traipsing the 12 hot kilometers to church.

At first the father refused to come inside. He stood outside and watched and listened. The following Sunday he ventured closer. After several weeks, not only did he come inside, but the stately old tribal gentleman stood before the congregation and spoke in broken Vietnamese. "I started coming because I wanted to see what you were doing and how you were treating my children. I wanted to know what made them come here every Sunday. When I saw you accepting them as part of your church, I knew there was something new and different here."

On that very same day he invited the church leaders to come to his village to witness the ridding of his house of spirit fetishes and to celebrate his embracing of the God of the Bible.

Throughout the following months, other tribal people accepted Christ and publicly announced their intent to follow Him. Soon they wanted to start their own worship services in the village. The Vietnamese congregation of believers offered to help them construct a chapel building and assist in paying a salary for a pastor. The bond of love between the two congregations grew and testified to the beautiful truth of Ephesians 2:14, that Christ does in fact destroy the walls that separate. For lack of a wall, God's love drew people into the kingdom, and a church was born.

5

Friday Fellowships

Mary Humphries

"So then, my brothers, because of God's great mercy to us I appeal to you:
Offer yourselves as a living sacrifice to God, dedicated to his service and
pleasing to him. This is the true worship that you should offer"
(Rom. 12:1 TEV).

The social event of our week in Saigon was the Friday Fellowship! Servicemen
and women, civilians, missionary families, and a few Vietnamese friends gathered at our house for supper every Friday night. Usually, between 50 and 75
persons were a part of this festive gathering. Picnic tables, supplied by a US
Army colonel and his unit, were in the front yard, along with several large bar-
becue grills. Frankly, I never knew until Friday morning what we were going
to serve. The menu was determined by what was available. Barbecued chick-
en, hamburgers, baked beans, and potato salad were typical fare, but perhaps
the favorite was pinto beans and corn bread. Some of the other foods (minus
the homemade touch) were available from time to time in the military dining
halls, but beans and corn bread were never to be found there.

I sometimes made banana pudding in my punch bowl. Other missionary
wives would bring a sumptuous array of homemade pies and cakes.

These fellowships were always a delight to the children. They tossed a foot-
ball or softball, went chasing through the yard playing hide-and-seek, or got
involved in a heated table game that would sometimes carry over from week
to week.

The children developed strong friendships with the servicemen. The GIs
brought the children candy, gum, and other hard-to-get items purchased at the
commissary. When the time came for men to rotate back to the States after their
tour in Vietnam, the children felt as if they were losing close friends. Our children
became very special to these men who had to be away from their own children
for a year; and I always felt that these fine, strong Christian men who also were
committed to serving their country were very good role models for our sons.

We seemed to grow into a large, close-knit extended family. As the men rotated to another tour of duty, our circle of friendships extended to the far corners of the earth. With the passing of time, we have lost contact with most of them; but occasionally we'll meet them here in the US. They will remember the fellowships and say, "I ate cherry pie at your house," or "I'll never forget Christmas dinner in your home that year I was separated from my family, halfway around the world."

Much of my time was spent cooking in a tiny space, a quite inadequate kitchen without air-conditioning or even a fan much of the time. It was always unbearably hot. One day as I was making pies and homemade rolls, perspiration dripped down my face and back. I said, "Lord, did you call me to the other side of the world to spend all of my time in the kitchen? Couldn't I have done this back in Texas?" I'm not sure exactly how He answered, but He did very strongly impress me to reply, "OK, Lord, if making pies and bread is what you want me to do, I will gladly do it." I came to believe that was the right response, for a short time later, I overheard my three-year-old daughter, Tracy, telling someone, "When I grow up, I'm going to be a mommy and make pies for army men."

However small the task may seem, it is important if it is performed in loving service to our Lord.

6

Harvest at Last

Priscilla Compher

"There is a large harvest, but few workers to gather it in. Pray to the owner
of the harvest that he will send out workers to gather in his harvest"
(Luke 10:2*b* TEV).

When we returned from our first furlough to start a second term of missionary service, we found the three churches we had started still functioning.
Educational programs were going well. A fourth church had been started in
the twin mountains section of Qui Nhon, as its Vietnamese name describes it.

With the American military pullout, thousands of people had lost their
jobs. The northern portion of the province had borne the burden of heavy
destruction from the 1972 fighting. Many residents who fled had never
returned. Many people lived in large refugee camps with little promise of
livelihood. People were selling the tin on their houses, electric lines, and light
bulbs to obtain money for food. Men and women were so desperate. Among
these were many Christians.

With the help of Gene Tunnell, a missionary assigned to social work, we
were allotted money to develop a Christian refugee community just south of
Qui Nhon, in front of the Cu Mong Pass. We resettled over 50 families from
two of the churches in Qui Nhon. We dug wells and built sod homes, a two-
room schoolhouse, and a church building. Initially, people gathered firewood
from the nearby mountains to use and to sell. They gathered brush for making brooms. For more long-range plans to help them economically, they planted mango seedlings. Each family was to be given pigs to raise.

Soon this project became known through the area. Invitations to share our
Christian faith were numerous, but we had no resources to follow up on most
of them.

A church was started in a government resettlement camp just south of Phu Tai at an abandoned American military base. Another church was birthed north of Qui Nhon just off of Highway 1.

Though trained leaders were few, seven churches now thrived. We depended greatly on help from the young people in the Qui Nhon Baptist Church, one lay preacher, and one strong administrator, a former Buddhist leader.

On most Sundays, Bob and I attended a worship service at all seven churches. We usually spoke in at least four of them. I could hear Jesus say those words as though He were standing in the center of Binh Dinh Province: "The harvest is ripe, the laborers are few. Talk to the Lord of the Harvest. Petition Him for laborers in the fields so ready for reaping."

When Gene Tunnell followed the call to Vietnam, he soon mobilized missionaries, Vietnamese, and American Christians stationed in Vietnam to do a better job of responding to the immense need in the country. The ministries spoke volumes to the recipients. A Christian Social Ministries Department was formed and officially received by the Vietnamese government as a worthy and vital arm of the networking needed to act and act quickly throughout the war-impaired society.

7

Praying on Automatic

Betty J. Merrell

"All of us hear them speaking in our own languages about
the great things that God has done!"
(Acts 2:11b TEV).

Spring 1967, Da Nang, South Vietnam. Co Nhi (Miss Nhi), our house helper was 17. On a cloudy afternoon she ran to me, obviously perturbed. "My parents were in a battle. Please may I go? I must hurry to get the last bus out to their village," she said.

She ran to get her money. Miss Nhi was not a believer in Jesus Christ. She worshiped the Buddhist way when she worshiped. I looked to the heavens and prayed: "*Lay Cha, chung con, o tren troi, Xin Cha, giup do Co Nhi va cha me cua co.*" (Please, our Father in heaven, help Nhi, and her father, and mother.) Suddenly, my mouth fell open with shock. I had automatically prayed in Vietnamese instead of English! I was drowned in a sense of awe. I fell on holy ground at this new way station on my missionary pilgrimage.

I imagined how many requests in America (and maybe by my Vietnamese Christian friends) had been directed to God on behalf of my Western tongue—that it could become Asian, that I could become all the things I needed to be to the Vietnamese so that some might be saved. The God of all communication answered their prayers in English and my prayer in Vietnamese that day. I was the recipient of God's grace, a grace that responds to all languages of prayer.

8

Recovering

Priscilla Compher

"If the Lord does not build the house, the work of the builders is useless;
if the Lord does not protect the city, it does no good for the
sentries to stand guard"
(Psalm 127:1 TEV).

While we were on vacation in Singapore, the offensive grinded away at nerves
and willpower, spawning fear and rumors. We returned to a one-room crowded guest unit in Saigon. The trauma of prevacation days in Qui Nhon hung
fresh in our memories, but lightened somewhat by the diversion of days out
of the country.

Bob decided to fly back to Qui Nhon to survey the situation. He flew on
the local commercial airlines, Air Vietnam. Only two people made up the pas-
senger list on the DC-3—Bob and an Australian journalist. Few wanted to go
to Qui Nhon during these days. Planes were full flying *out* of Qui Nhon.

He found the city quiet—almost like a ghost town. Most people had fled
further south. The only activity was in the schoolyard where thousands of
refugees were now living. They had fled there from other areas in the province,
areas even less secure, but they could not afford to travel any farther south.

Bob assessed damage at our activity center and the three churches. All the
library books in our second library were gone as were the sewing machines
from the tailoring class and the chairs in one of the churches. People had
begun living in the church at Phu Tai. The leaders of the different churches,
thinking the Communists would overrun our area, had taken the church and
activity center furniture with them as they moved away—to sell. We never discovered exactly what happened to the library books. Food from our house had
been taken, but the house had not been looted otherwise.

Bob talked with the American military advisers to the province officials.
They reported fighting still heavy in the central part of the province, and the
outcome was unknown. Between the Communist forces and the city of Qui

Nhon was a division of Korean soldiers. The advisers did not think the enemy forces could get through them.

Bob caught a ride on an American military cargo plane and returned to Saigon for us.

Before long B-52 raids flown from American bases in other countries stopped the enemy advance. People began returning to Binh Dinh Province and into the city of Qui Nhon. This dangerous period for our family and others was over.

Heavy destruction lay strewn in most of the province. Several hundred thousand refugees still lived in camps throughout the province.

For us personally, the damage was to relationships with the leaders in the churches. We had worked hard to help them understand the Christian faith, to develop them as leaders. They now returned, ashamed of their reactive behavior, but too embarrassed to face openly what they had done.

We recovered some of the furniture and sewing machines. We never reopened the second library. Our next-door neighbor, Mr. Hoi, helped to recover the building at Phu Tai. He wrote to the military authorities thanking the people who had served as caretakers of the church building during the period of turmoil and reported that those who had legal access to the building were again ready to use it. Thus, he tactfully handled the situation. Since the leader of the group who had taken control of the building was a soldier, higher military authorities ordered him and his relatives to leave under threat of being transferred to a most dangerous assignment.

Our Qui Nhon Baptist Church building was finished our last year of this term and the Christians began worshiping there.

With our second four-year term completed in Qui Nhon, we left South Vietnam for our second furlough in the US. The Lord had used us to help start three churches. Each church had an adequate building. Ongoing ministries included the lending library, the sewing school, and a kindergarten which had been developed in the Qui Nhon church.

The Lord had blessed His work and us. We looked forward to our fourth child for I was five months pregnant as we flew homeward by way of the Middle East and Europe.

9

Singing the Good News

Dottie Hayes

"Christ's message in all its richness must live in your hearts. Teach and instruct one another with all wisdom. Sing psalms, hymns, and sacred songs; sing to God with thanksgiving in your hearts"
(Col. 3:16 TEV).

When Herman, Hope, and I returned to Vietnam from our second furlough, we were asked by our Mission to begin work in the delta city of Can Tho, 75 miles south of Saigon. We had left Paul and Tim in the US for college, and we were finding the separation very difficult. The new assignment also meant I would be teaching Hope at home. Many new adjustments awaited us, but we also found a peace in knowing this was God's will for us. We soon found a house and settled in.

Hope became aware of the small art shop next door to our house almost immediately. One day she stopped by the shop and met the owner. Hope ran back home and asked me to go over and meet her new friend. We soon learned that five of the owner's nieces were living with her in order to go to school. She asked if we would please teach the girls English. This new contact opened many doors for us in our new work.

Hope and I began to make plans to teach the girls. The classes would have to be taught at night, and we invited the girls to bring their friends. The first night 14 girls arrived. We gave them a simple test to decide the level of English we needed to teach. We organized a beginner level with Hope as their teacher. Hope was a grown-up aged 10 at this time! I taught the higher-level class. We had such fun that night getting acquainted with our new friends.

We met once a week in our home and soon averaged 25. The study expanded to include cooking, table setting, and singing as well as other suggestions they brought.

The girls were among the first to attend our worship services. They always carried their English books. Later I learned this was the only way they were

94

allowed to come because their parents understood they were attending English class.

During the second year of our English classes, we wanted to do something to make a greater impact for the gospel with these students. We remembered hearing the musical *Good News* while on furlough. Because our students loved to sing, we decided to try to get copies of the musical and teach it to them in English, explaining the meaning of each song in Vietnamese. Soon after our decision, we received a letter from a church women's missions group in the US asking us for a project—something they could do to help us in our work. We suggested that our greatest need was for their prayers and if possible they could collect about 12 used copies of *Good News* and send them as soon as possible. Within two months this wonderful group sent 25 copies, some used and others new. They were as excited as we were!

A young American soldier stationed in Can Tho was teaching Hope to play the piano. When we told him about our dream to teach our students the musical, he volunteered to be our pianist. God was providing all we needed, so we had to get to work. And work we did! The students loved it and learned quickly. One night during practice they suggested we present the musical to their parents, a wonderful idea which Hope and I had already had. It was extra special coming from them.

The day came when we all felt comfortable enough about the musical to send invitations to their parents and friends. The musical would be presented at our house.

Our big night finally arrived and we were all atwitter. The girls were beautiful in their lovely white *ao dais* (long Vietnamese dresses). Seventy people came and filled our living/dining room. The girls sang superbly. One gave a short explanation of each song in Vietnamese to be sure their parents understood. Their favorite song was "Sunday Child" and they sang it as well as any choir back in the US. Many heard the gospel for the first time that night. What a grand finale for us as we prepared to take up a new ministry in Saigon. We often wonder where these girls are now—still in Vietnam or in some other part of the world. God knows and He will use His Word sung in those songs.

The text of Western songs differed from the usual music in Vietnam. The often upbeat messages with rhythms and melodies to match were loved and accepted by the Vietnamese people. They sang them alongside their more plaintiff folk tunes that often cast upon the winds the tragedies of their lives, note by note.

10

The Blessing

Beth Goad

"For by the sacrificial death of Christ we are set free, that is, our sins are forgiven. How great is the grace of God, which he gave to us in such large measure! In all his wisdom and insight God did what he had purposed, and made known to us the secret plan he had already decided to complete by means of Christ. This plan, which God will complete when the time is right, is to bring all creation together, everything in heaven and on earth, with Christ as head"
(Eph. 1:7-10 TEV).

Language study was tough! Every day, I felt an elevated need for prayer as I struggled to learn the Vietnamese language. Though I was sure my tongue would never talk it, the Lord heard my prayers and provided facility.

Part of God's help came in the graceful form of my Vietnamese sister in Christ, Hoang Bich, who tutored me in the Vietnamese language every afternoon. I had completed one year's work in our language school. I was schoolteacher to our children in the mornings; I was being taught Vietnamese in the afternoons.

Bich and I had become acquainted at the language school where she taught. Our relationship was just business at first. I needed a tutor; she needed additional work.

A beautiful surprise lay in store for both of us. The light of our Father's love began to illuminate our similarities—personality, temperament, training, family. And our differences—language, culture, skin, eyes, hair—began to fade into insignificance. Often we expressed mutual surprise. She would tell me of some characteristic of Vietnamese women which she thought unique to them. I would reply, "But, American women are like that too!"

As we studied, the Lord gave to each of us an understanding of the other that far surpassed our language abilities. Though she had accepted Christ as her Savior years before, she had yet to begin to enjoy the new life that was hers in Christ. As she helped me learn to express myself in her language, I had the joy of helping her understand truths more clearly as a redeemed child of God.

I learned, quite by accident, how significant the word *redeemed* was to her. A girl in Vietnam quickly learned that life would have been much better for her had she been born a boy. Vietnamese traditional feelings toward the births of girls and boys could roughly be paralleled to some attitudes in the Old Testament concerning sorrows and good fortune. Sorrow is surely evidence of sin somewhere! Good fortune is the smile of God. Likewise, in Vietnam, the birth of a daughter was met with little rejoicing—even at times with the attitude that they're not pleasing the spirits. The birth of a son was deemed *phuoc*, the Vietnamese word for good fortune or blessing.

A son, especially the eldest—the prince of the family—carried many responsibilities, but also enjoyed many privileges. His actions as he grew up were accepted with great leniency, without fear of bringing disgrace on the family. Not so with a daughter. She walked a tightrope of traditional do's and don'ts and often grew up with a heavy load of being *not OK*.

One Sunday in church, the pastor's text was Romans 8:16-17. As I read the verses in my Vietnamese Bible, I discovered a word with which I was not familiar: *ke-tu*. I looked it up in the dictionary. It meant *heir*.

The next day as we began our study, I asked Bich to read that passage with me, to make sure that I understood the meaning of the new word. She read the words silently, then looked up at me, her eyes full of tears. Speaking with difficulty, she said, "You don't yet understand all of the significance expressed here in the Vietnamese language. *Ke-tu* does mean *heir*, but it has peculiar reference to the eldest son as heir with all the attendant privileges which are his."

She continued, "That means because Christ has bought (redeemed) me and I am a child of God, I am no longer an 'evidence of sin'—but I am elevated to being an heir and blessing on the level with the eldest son!"

11

The Chain Reaction

Rachel James

"Then he sent them out to preach the Kingdom of God and to heal the sick" (Luke 9:2 TEV).

It all started when I was 14, on the day I walked forward in a revival service to present myself to the Lord to go wherever He would lead me as a missionary nurse. Thus started the pilgrimage that led through Duke University School of Nursing and landed me in South Vietnam.

By 1962, when I arrived in Vietnam, I got off the plane as a wife and a mother of three small children. During those early years, I had very little opportunity to practice my calling as a nurse.

One day in the summer of 1968, an army chaplain friend stood at the door with a young medical doctor. He introduced him as Dr. Leo Record, the army medical doctor for the chaplains' battalion. Dr. Record responded, "I am a doctor, a Christian, and I will be in Vietnam for a year. What can I do to help?"

Little did the chaplain know that this was an answer to years of prayer. This one introduction triggered a chain reaction which led to years of Christian medical work in and around the churches in the greater Saigon area. Within one week a medical clinic was opened in a small chapel. Within weeks clinics were begun in two additional locations. The training of a number of Christians was conducted to help them know how to witness to the large number of Vietnamese who waited for hours to be seen by the American doctor and missionary nurse. The practical experience of working closely with this doctor and the constant training under his tutelage resulted in my taking special nurse practitioner training on our next furlough. When I returned to South Vietnam from that furlough in 1973, the American military had withdrawn from South Vietnam. The loss of Christian army doctors made it difficult to continue the medical work.

It was difficult, but not impossible. An army canteen vehicle was purchased by the Christian Social Ministries Department of the Baptist Mission under the leadership of Gene Tunnell. Its stainless steel interior made it ideal for conversion into a mobile clinic.

When application was made to the Ministry of Health, they granted permission based on my experience and special training to operate the mobile clinic with some limitations due to my status as a nurse. With this assurance, the mobile clinic was outfitted for the road. Just as we began the new medical work, the Ministry of Health changed its decision and ordered that a medical doctor must accompany the mobile clinic. Hope seemed lost for a continuation of the ministry—but then a miracle arrived.

At a meeting of nongovernmental aid organizations, missionary Gene Tunnell met a Vietnamese woman, a medical doctor. He shared with her our need for a doctor to work with the mobile unit. She expressed an interest and he introduced her to me. As we discussed the ministry, she became excited and started talking about the possibilities. She revealed that she was a Catholic, but had interned at the North Carolina Baptist Hospital in Winston-Salem, North Carolina. She knew what our mission in the name of Jesus was all about. In a discussion about what kind of clothes to wear during clinic ministry, she asked, "Do we need to wear a badge saying that we are Baptists?" I said, "No, we have a large sign on the outside of the vehicle telling who we are."

In early April 1975, just prior to the Communist victory over South Vietnam, it was announced that medical personnel were greatly needed by the Communist forces. Suddenly the threat of kidnapping of medical personnel became very real. Few Western women were visible on the streets of South Vietnam's cities during those days.

Missionary Celia Moore, who helped dispense medicines during the clinics, and I made the decision not to ride in the mobile unit any longer. American women were just too tempting a target especially in a medical vehicle. We drove in a private car a distance behind the unit to and from the clinic sites. At the last mobile clinic prior to the fall of Saigon, we were on-site at Phu Tho Hoa Baptist Church on the outskirts of the city. Suddenly, a loud noise interrupted the silence inside the clinic unit. We thought a gunshot had hit the vehicle. But an immediate investigation revealed instead that a child had thrown a rock against the side of the unit. The terror we felt awakened us with a jolt to the anxiety and tension which existed unrecognized within us. The years of living in the midst of crisis and war had taught us to ignore such fear in order to continue to minister effectively in the name of Jesus.

On the day that I was forced to leave Saigon, the mobile clinic was making its way into the needy areas. The committed Christian Vietnamese woman doctor was continuing that ministry begun so many years before with the introduction of a young American Christian army doctor who during a brief tenure in a foreign land wanted to be of service to the Lord and to the Vietnamese people.

12

The Miracle of Healing

Rosalie Beck

"Lord, heal me and I will be completely well; rescue me and
I will be perfectly safe. You are the one I praise!"
(Jer. 17:14 TEV).

I majored in biology at the University of California at San Diego and worked
as a biochemist for two years before becoming a short-term missionary. I knew
science and had a healthy respect for it. Growing up in a Christian home, I
also had a healthy respect for God's ability to do miracles, even the miracle of
healing. In Vietnam, my scientific skepticism ran headlong into my bedrock
faith in God's omnipotence.

Thanksgiving was a time for the missionary families to gather in the
mountains of Da Lat and spend the holiday in a spiritual retreat. A retreat
usually consisted of worship, Bible study, some planning, a lot of tennis, and
Forty-two (a Texas mutation of dominoes); but in 1974 the agenda changed
somewhat.

Shirley and Avery Willis, missionaries in Indonesia, arrived in Da Lat with
their assignment: help the Vietnam Mission move toward spiritual renewal.
Avery was serving as the president of the seminary in Indonesia and his family
had been on the field since 1964. He was working on perfecting an Indonesian
guide which eventually became *MasterLife*.

Over the Thanksgiving weekend, Avery led the Mission family through
steps of cleansing and empowerment. He guided us in seeking a clear conscience before the Lord, asking for and giving forgiveness. The first evening he
talked about the need for a clear conscience if we are to petition God seriously about anything. He took God's Word and showed us that asking for forgiveness and giving up grudges is necessary. The Spirit moved among us and
we began to confess grudges and ask for forgiveness. Some slights had been

incurred in the early days of the Mission's work. Some were new. But as the evening progressed, each person looked into his or her own life to acknowledge what God did not want there. That undesirable part was exposed to the light of confession and the healing of forgiveness. From that session on, the event's title became Spiritual Retreat.

I cannot remember another time in my two years with the missionaries when so much praying and spiritual discussion took place among the men and women who had followed God's call to Vietnam. Da Lat was our fellowship, fun, and relaxation capital; yet, this time we hung together, talking in small groups or moving alone for a special time with God—in preference to the usual games, physical or spiritual.

The conference center where we met included a lounge area. In the late evenings some of us gathered there to talk quietly or just pray among friends. The third night of the retreat, as some of us gathered, Priscilla Tunnell asked to speak. Prissy shared that she had been ill with an ear infection that had ruptured one eardrum, might rupture the other, and the condition was complicated with the growth of a fungus. She explained, "The medicine that is treating the infection is feeding the fungus and the medicine that is treating the fungus is feeding the infection." For months she had lived with a loud ringing and great pain. She needed further treatment but air travel was impossible with her problem. I was aware of some of her story, but the amount of pain she was dealing with took me by surprise. What made the whole narrative so tragic was that Prissy was the Mission's prime music resource person. Though trained and gifted in voice, Prissy had not been able to sing for months.

As Prissy finished her story, I wondered why she'd told it in such detail. Then, she knelt in the middle of the floor and asked, with a shaky voice and bowed head, that we pray for her healing. I was dumbfounded! I had never experienced anything like that, but her request seemed logical and right.

Sherry Bengs stood and walked up to Prissy, singing "Amazing Grace." Sherry placed her hands on Prissy's head and stood for a moment praying as the rest of us joined in the song. Each person in turn, sometimes by twos, went to stand by Prissy and touch her with love and faith. After we had all prayed for her healing, we sat staring at one another, at the floor, at the ceiling. I felt embarrassed. What does one do at such a time? More importantly, was Prissy healed? Or were we fools?

After a few minutes of silence, Prissy raised her head. Tears streamed down her face. She looked at each of us, opened her mouth, and sang one of the most beautiful arrangements of "The Lord's Prayer" that I have ever heard. When she finished, all were weeping. She said that for the first time in months she could hear and there was no pain or ringing. She rushed out to find Gene, her husband, to tell him what had happened.

When Prissy and Gene returned to Saigon, she kept her next appointment with the doctor. Now it was his turn to be dumbfounded. Not only was the infection and fungus gone, but the eardrum showed no signs of ever being ruptured.

Why is it so amazing that the Lord would heal our relationships and Prissy's ear? When we are right with God, many forms of healing can occur. Of the two I witnessed in Da Lat, I think the restoration of relationships left the greater impression on my mind. Those renewed ties allowed the missionaries who made up the Mission to accomplish incredible tasks in the power of God—actions that prepared us, the Vietnamese Christians, and those yet to be born again for what was to come. The Lord moved in a great way in the months following the retreat. We were able to participate with the Lord in His mighty work in expanding dimensions because He knew the country would be closed to missionary endeavors the next year.

Our last years in Vietnam were years of harvest. Hundreds started their pilgrimages of faith that would take them through hardships of days ahead. Missionaries turned toward a focus on preparation for the Second Coming of Jesus Christ.

13

The Miracle of Partnering

Barbara Wigger

"There is no difference between the man who plants and the man who waters; God will reward each one according to the work he has done. For we are partners working together for God, and you are God's field" (1 Cor. 3:8-9 TEV).

Our four years in Vietnam were wonderfully happy years, mostly due to the people with whom we lived and worked—the Vietnamese people and our American missionary colleagues. We were in Vietnam to live among those gracious Southeast Asian people who had lived in war conditions throughout their lives. Sometimes we were able to meet their needs. Sometimes those needs were physical—Anh Tu's (brother four) was.

While living in Da Lat a gentle-spirited woman named Chi Ba worked in our home. She had worked previously for several missionary families and during one of those terms of service, she had become a Christian.

Several months after our move to Saigon, we were surprised to find Chi Ba at our front gate one Sunday afternoon. Her husband, Anh Tu, was with her. After hurried greetings they poured out a story which we heard frequently in that country. Anh Tu worked as a gardener which meant, in part, literally manicuring lawns by hand with a small tool. One afternoon he was squatting on the front lawn cutting the grass. He heard a plane overhead. He looked up and then returned to his task, but soon felt a warm sensation in his jaw—and discovered blood when he touched his face. While looking up at the plane, a stray bullet had come from *out of nowhere* across the valley and lodged in his lower jaw. He was taken to the Province Hospital where he remained for several weeks. Doctors x-rayed and examined, but refused to operate. The location of the bullet was so precarious they were afraid to attempt its removal.

In desperation Chi Ba brought her weakened husband to Saigon and asked if there was anything we could do to help. My mind flashed to a recent dinner guest we had entertained in our home, Colonel Jack Meredith. We had met

Jack only recently; however, his family were members of the US church where I had served on the staff. When he left home for Vietnam, his church staff gave him our address and suggested he contact us. He did. We invited him to our home and got acquainted one evening. As Jack prepared to leave and return to his base, he had turned and handed us his business card, saying, "If there is anything I can do for you, please call."

On that Sunday afternoon with Chi Ba and Anh Tu sitting in our living room, I went in search of that card. I called Jack to explain Anh Tu's condition. The next morning, with Colonel Meredith's instructions in hand, David took Anh Tu to an oral surgeon at Third Field Hospital just minutes from our home. Within a few hours, Anh Tu left that hospital compound clutching the menacing bullet in his hand, and literally leaped and praised God.

Anh Tu and Chi Ba had experienced a miracle of God's love through a stranger's faith and the compassionate response of American military personnel on duty in Southeast Asia.

14

When Are You Going to Do the Rest of the Story?

Priscilla Tunnell

"For our gifts of knowledge and of inspired messages are only partial; but
when what is perfect comes, then what is partial will disappear"
(1 Cor. 13:9-10 TEV).

I couldn't believe my ears! They really wanted to try! They thought if we
worked hard enough we could learn it! "It" was the Christmas portion of
Handel's *Messiah!* Our choir had 30 voices—when they were all in the country and not on alert, or out preaching, teaching, sick, or otherwise busy at
their main reason for being in Vietnam.

The 30 voices came from several different countries representing five Asian
countries, as well as the US and Canada. Many could not read music or even
speak English clearly, but all were excited. Now we had to find the music.
Thanks to several churches in the States we collected enough copies for each
person to have a personal copy. This was important because everyone had to
learn how to pronounce the words in the same way, so making notes on the
music was essential.

Each worked individually, especially during times when curfews were
early. When we could practice together, the sound was splendid, full and rich.
Not only did we learn the music, but we discussed how we would use this presentation to glorify the Lord. It was decided that the best way was to be sure
there were people in attendance to experience the majesty of the music and
the story it told. We decided on three presentations in three days, each in a
different setting. Posters were made and distributed for each concert. Our first
presentation was to be downtown in Saigon at the Vietnamese-American
Association (VAA) auditorium.* Our posters were proudly hung all around
the area of the VAA hoping they would stir interest.

Attendance at a concert in Vietnam was always preceded by some preliminary study preparing you for what you were about to hear. This was a little gift that the Vietnamese culture gave me. So, the Vietnamese young people were busy going to libraries and bookstores looking for information about the *Messiah* and Handel.

One day the United States Information Service at the embassy called our Mission office asking if we had anything they could give to the Vietnamese who were asking for information. Of course we answered in the affirmative and then began scratching our heads as to what we were going to provide. Then came the plan. We printed up a half sheet introducing the composer Handel and some background information about the musical composition the *Messiah*. We pasted them in the front of Vietnamese New Testaments marking them with verses about Jesus, the Messiah. We prepared several boxes of New Testaments and took them to the United States embassy.

Before we knew it, the time had come for the marathon weekend of performances. Musically we were ready, physically we looked handsome in our outfits, and through much prayer we were spiritually prepared; but we were not prepared for the response we received.

The Vietnamese-American Association building was packed. People were seated on the floor and hanging in all the windows. Officials put a microphone outside for the scores of people who could not get near the building. We sang with such inspiration that words pale in the telling. The Lord anointed and multiplied our efforts.

After the performance, most of us ended up with a line of Vietnamese people asking questions and wanting to know more. We were able to answer most of the questions, but the one we had trouble with was, When are you going to do the rest of the story?

The performance at the American Military Chapel went well and so did the one at the English-speaking church. But neither was as inspired as when we sang to hundreds of people hearing the gospel for the first time. We hoped the opportunity would come for us to sing the Crucifixion and Easter portion, so we could put out posters saying, here is the rest of the story.

*The Vietnamese-American Association was an organization popular with Vietnamese as it provided channels for involvement with the arts and sciences and other enrichment opportunities. Students and professional personnel especially frequented VAA facilities and utilized resources.

15

998 Tongues to Go

Beth Goad

"Sing to the Lord, all the world! Worship the Lord with joy;
come before him with happy songs!"
(Psalm 100:1-2 TEV).

I heard the song again one morning in Manila while making my bed and
remembered the revelation of that Sunday morning in February 1975. We
were singing at Trinity Baptist Church in Saigon.

O for a thousand tongues to sing
My great Redeemer's praise,
The glories of my God and King,
The triumphs of his grace!

How much I had sung those words! How little I had understood what I was
singing! But that Sunday, in one instant of remembering I comprehended the
meaning, and for me that grand old hymn was forever enriched and
entrenched in my growing.

Ken and I had been studying Vietnamese for 18 months, and though not
yet proficient, we were beginning to communicate. After the initial year's cur-
riculum in the language school, I had chosen to concentrate on the "Religious
Supplement"—terminology of a more abstract nature, words used in describ-
ing love, friendship, caring—things of that nature. It also included study of
the Bible in Vietnamese and learning to pray in that language.

That momentary flashback had speeded me back to the Christmas Eve just
past—our second in Da Lat. During that Christmas season we unpacked deco-
rations, and trimmed our house and tree. In between we packed books, linens,
pans, and dishes for the move to Saigon after the holidays.

Christmas, with its attendant hustle and bustle, can be fatal. But this time,
from the first carol sung, I was aware of a spirit, a feeling as warm and uplifting

as my memories of childhood Christmases. It seemed a bit incongruous in the muddle of moving, but I didn't stop to analyze, I just enjoyed!

On Christmas Eve we met for a time of worship and fellowship with the young people of Hoi Thanh Bap-tit Trung-Tin (Faith Baptist Church), newly constituted in Da Lat. As we read in Vietnamese the prophecies in Isaiah, and their fulfillment in Matthew and Luke, and sang the messages of Christmas, joy was piled upon joy.

The celebration of Christmas in English stirred within me on a somewhat subconscious level, but experiencing the old familiar story in a new language was like hearing it for the first time ever. Layers of God's amazing grace came alive with new depths of meaning created by the Vietnamese words. My joy leaped higher as the young people prayed, and as I understood their words of praise and adoration to Him Whose birthday we celebrated.

My merry Christmas doubled. For the first time in my life I read the Scriptures, sang the songs, and prayed the prayers of the season in two tongues. The entire Christmas season was twice as wonderful. And I thought, *Now! Just 998 to go, until I have the "thousand tongues to sing my great Redeemer's praise!"*

That Sunday morning in Saigon, as I was singing those words, I began to imagine with Charles Wesley what singing God's praises in 1,000 languages might mean.

Our Daughters

1
A Nine-year-old's Room with a View

Hope Hayes Hudson

"We know that in all things God works for good with those who love him" (Rom. 8:28a TEV).

"Daddy, do you hear firecrackers? Can we go up to the rooftop and watch them? Please?"

That was the last thing I remember asking my dad before he told us to go to our rooms and stay there! What was going on? Why couldn't I go up to the roof and look? Mom explained very calmly that those were not firecrackers, they were gunshots. But we need not be afraid; we should stay calm. Well, I stayed as calm as a nine-year-old could stay. I got under my bed! I remember telling Mom at some point, "Don't be afraid, Jesus is going to be with us."

Those *firecrackers* seemed awfully close. In fact, they were actually just across the street. The next day, after a sleepless night for Mom and Dad, we discovered that the Vietcong had dug an underground tunnel from an area across the street from our house to the horse track. There they were launching their own little war inside the war.

A few days after this *war* had started, American GIs came down the street with tanks and actually tore down the wall directly in front of our house. I remember being struck in amazement by the tanks and the damage they could inflict to a wall. From our front room windows we watched the wall come down. It was an awesome scene for a nine-year-old!

By the third day the Americans had everything under control and we talked with the GIs who came to see if we were all right. They had heard that an American family lived there. Seeing that we were fine, one soldier asked my mom for an aspirin. I guess tearing down walls can cause discomfort.

My mom barbecued some chicken over charcoal because we did not have any electricity and we enjoyed sharing it with the GIs. Even though all of this was going on all around me, I actually had no fear. My parents were the ones to be thanked, as they kept everything functioning on a normal routine. Looking back, I realize that the Lord was taking care of everything in His own way through each of us—just as He promised!

On the fifth day of the siege we were evacuated to Thailand where I spent the last half of my third grade in a new school. But that is another story.

2

Can Tho, Vietnam

Hope Hayes Hudson

"I thank my God for you every time I think of you;
and every time I pray for you all"
(Phil. 1:3-4*a* TEV).

My family first moved to Can Tho, a city south of Saigon, in 1969 to begin new missions work. Can Tho was a friendly city. Our first friends were our next-door neighbors who owned an art shop. Mom and I joined together to teach English to the owner. It was great doing missions work with my mom.

Soon I found a new friend. Her name was Trinh. She was my saving force during that time, my closest friend and confidante. We did everything together except school. She went to a Vietnamese school and my mom taught me at home. After school we would meet at her house across the street and down the little lane, or we would meet at mine and play with dolls or just visit and talk. Sometimes I would spend the night with her on her wooden bed under a mosquito net and other times she would stay with me, sleeping on my soft bed under a ceiling fan. I have no idea what has happened to Trinh since 1975, but I still think of her and those precious memories of Can Tho. Time and distance cannot rob me of these memories.

3

Emerging Memories

Hope Hayes Hudson

"I will remember your great deeds, Lord; I will recall the wonders
you did in the past. I will think about all that you have done;
I will meditate on all your mighty acts"
(Psalm 77:11-12 TEV).

The year was 1975. The day I don't remember. Time has blocked it out, but time has not blocked the feelings of loss. They are as real to me as they were the day I heard Vietnam was no longer free. I was distraught. I hurt all over. The loss of *my* country was a bizarre nightmare, hard to believe. I was not with my parents. I was in boarding school in Taiwan. The loss of Vietnam became more real to me as time went by.

Even now I feel pain deep within. I realize that some very special feelings I have for Vietnam have been suppressed for years and are beginning to reemerge. I experience feelings of loss like a loved one gone forever or a special friend who has died. I deal with this gripping need to pull it all back just as it was before, real and alive.

4

Eyes Not Quite Round

C'Anne Moore Wofford

"Come to me, all of you who are tired from carrying heavy loads,
and I will give you rest. Take my yoke and put it on you, and learn from me,
because I am gentle and humble in spirit; and you will find rest"
(Matt. 11:28-29 TEV).

In the middle of June
In the middle of traffic
In the midst of the eighties,
Windows rolled down
Warm breeze passing through?
Or the sound of the Stones
Or the smell of the diesel . . .
That reminds me of you.

Takes me back to the sixties.

Too young to know
Quite where I belong;
Too young to *not* know
Who's going to Hell.
Young life passing through
Struggles the same
Fights to retain?
That reminds me of you.

I miss you yet fear you.
The questions unanswered
The answers unasked
In this world far away.

Incomplete passing through
Still missing some parts
Though He fills the hole . . .
That reminds me of you.

Takes me back to my home.

The rumble excites me
running to wave to
smiling GIs rolling by,
Staying up counting flares
The sky passing through.
The rattle of glass,
My parents in prayer,
Still remind me of you.

This was my childhood home though I wonder if I ever felt a part of it. I am separated from those memories by a thick tongue and a round eye. And yet, these are the same things that had separated me from my people—or perhaps, that was a round tongue and a thick eye, having seen too many things to keep my mouth shut. For some reason I would not trade who I am, but I would trade some knowledge of myself. I have learned to believe in God though I don't always believe in some who share Him. I was fortunate enough to see a world where other gods ruled, and when I came back to *the* God I was truly amazed at grace.

How can I share what I know and what I still don't understand? My childhood was a childhood—happiness, adventure, games with friends, love letters, Barbie dolls, and GI Joes. It was a little different from the average American's—a lot more shots (from burly army nurses!), C-rations for campout food, picking up live bullets at the airport, tear gas bombs thrown in the schoolyard. And I missed out on *Leave It to Beaver*, but I have overcome that scar! I learned to accept the unaccepted, to cheer for the underdog, and to be proud of my heritage even when it makes me weep from shame.

This is a story that won't go away because it was not just an experience; it was, and is, my life. It is viewing life, from eyes not quite round.

5

Identity Crisis

Deborah James Winans

"The Lord is all I have, and so in him I put my hope.
The Lord is good to everyone who trusts in him, So it is best for us to wait
in patience . . . And it is best to learn this patience in our youth"
(Lam. 3:24-27 TEV).

After South Vietnam came under Communist rule in 1975 and a year of unexpected furlough in the States, I returned to my high school in Taiwan where I had previously boarded, Morrison Christian Academy.

One of my classes was senior ethics. At the end of September we were assigned a paper to write titled, "Who Am I?" The teacher instructed that we were not to give pat answers such as name, rank, and serial number. Being a procrastinator, I put off the writing until fall break.

On the train going to my parents' house I began to think about what I would write. I could come up with nothing. I began to feel some anxiety as I realized I didn't know who I was! All of my identity was wrapped in the package that I was Deborah James, daughter of Sam and Rachel James, "missionaries' kid" in South Vietnam, 17 years old. Most of my identity had been stripped away with the loss of my country. I was American on the outside, but certainly not on the inside. Who was I?

I sought counsel from my dad. As I cried and shared my inner fear and emptiness, he caused me to see something that would help me for the rest of my life.

If you take a pot—a large one—and boil away all the outer layer (name, parents, rank, and serial number) including my church identity (organizations, choirs), what is left in the very center is love. Not the love that I would have for my parents, as special as it is, or a boyfriend. Not the love of possessions, which is temporary. But the love that God had for me. Love so great that He sent His only Son, Jesus, to die for me. That's a love that cannot be taken away, he said. It has surpassed thousands of years. Paul was persecuted for it. Stephen was stoned for it. Yet it goes right on. That same love I accepted as a child.

I realized then that it would never matter where I was from or what my name and age were. What mattered was, and is, that I am a child of the Almighty, Omnipotent God. My identity lay in who I was in Him. That would continue.

The Lord gave me a Scripture verse that became my life verse during my college years that followed: "Love bears all things, believes all things, hopes all things, and endures all things" (1 Cor. 13:7 KJV). I could endure anything with Him.

Henceforth—my identity is in Christ and His being crucified, resurrected, and risen for my eternal life.

6

I Have Heard the Dogs of War

C'Anne Moore Wofford

"So put on God's armor now! Then when the evil day comes, you will be able to resist the enemy's attacks; and after fighting to the end, you will still hold your ground" (Eph. 6:13 TEV).

I have heard the dogs of war
howling in the night.
Awakened by the new year moon
crimson from the fight.

Stars are blocked by flash of light
dancing 'round and 'round
Are they hiding yesterday?
Will the day be found?

Morning holds a glowing sun,
laughter, games, and fun
rumbling ground, thundering sky
Still my smile is not undone.

Thunder hides the bomber's roar
rain encircles peace,
tiny drops are friends of mine
drowning out disease.

I have lived a thousand lives
in my thirty years
holding those dogs at bay
through facets of my tears.

7

Journal Entry
Deborah James Winans

"The thought of my pain, my homelessness, is bitter poison. Yet hope
returns when I remember . . . The Lord's unfailing love and mercy still
continue, Fresh as the morning, as sure as the sunrise"
(Lam. 3:19,21-23 TEV).

September 3, 1975, four months after "the fall," Highland Springs, Virginia, 16
years old.

"The spring and summer of 1975 seemed a period of traumatic experiences.
Tenseness, horror, fright, and uncertainty describe those months for me, our
family, and the people of South Vietnam.

"As time went by, with its unknown expectations, the risk grew too great
for us to linger any longer there. With great fear, regret, and many mixed emotions, my family and other missionaries left—becoming refugees, leaving
everything behind except what could be carried out in a suitcase . . . we no
longer had a place to call home, nothing left to our name that we had before
Vietnam or had collected for 17 years in Vietnam. We had to come back to
America, which we children knew hardly anything about.

"Now it seems like everything makes us long for home. Life is now one
emotional rollercoaster as the grief strikes and the tears flow. We begin to realize that Vietnam can no longer be called home. We can no longer communicate with those dear friends we so love. We live in a world now where everything strikes within us a little fear."

8

Ka-cushes and 222s

Diane Davis Casebier

"Lord God, my savior, I cry out all day, and at night I come before you.
Hear my prayer; listen to my cry for help!" (Psalm 88:1-2 TEV).

Waking up midsleep to screaming ka-cushing sounds
Murmurs of neighbors stepping down for cover to the ground.
Sirens wailing charging the streets
Shouts, "Is it over?" fueling for relief.

Putting heads under beds where the rest would not fit,
Holding hands with sisters praying for death swift
Or not being torn alive by shrapnel piece.

Smoky, dusty, powdery fall
Stuffing up your nose . . .
Wondering where the next would hit
Clenching teeth and petrified limbs.

Then remembering when rockets rained
Being called to sleep together again
On mattresses piled on the floor
When the rare occasional air-conditioner roared
To soothe children to sleep
To drown ka-cushing screams.

Then finally learning through the years
My parents answer to our fears,
"Those are not close; go back to sleep."
So trustingly to bed we would creep.

Ka-cushes are rockets; 222s were artillery.

9

Recollections
Deborah James Winans

"Be thankful in all circumstances"
(1 Thess. 5:18a TEV).

Recollections One
Busy streets, bicycles, motorcycles, cyclos and taxicabs, crowded buses; men
hanging on the outside
The smell of diesel fuel
Bumpy, pot-holed roads—unattended
Marketplaces; hundreds selling their wares
People everywhere—too many to comprehend
Women clutching purses tightly under the arm
Children touching the skin and calling, "*My! My, oi!*" (American, American!)
Children with outstretched hands begging for any coin that may be given
Children begging to wash a car for an extra coin
Smiling faces pushing to get in front of the camera
Groups of children dancing and singing their favorite songs
Beautiful smells of flowers on "Flower Street"
Funny smells of *durian* being sold*
Stinky smells of the garbage dump down the lane
Sweet smell of *plumaria* behind a missionary's house**
Sounds of machine gun fire late at night
Bombs dropping in the distance, rattling the windows
Horns honking everywhere, all the time
Noises of war and noises of life. One gets used to it.

Recollections Two
Picking *guava* to eat and *plumaria* for leis behind the Davis house
The Hayes house flooded to our knees after a monsoon rain
Red and orange records of the Beatles that belong to Paul and Tim Hayes

Terry Moore playing his guitar
Aunt Ida Davis and Aunt Mary Humphries teaching Sunday School
Aunt Olive Allen leading three of us in GAs
Mission meetings and Thanksgiving retreats
Uncle Lewis singing "Here Is My Life"
Sitting in awe of the high schoolers returning home for summer or Christmas
Cindy Davis telling ghost stories in a darkened room
Cab rides to the market or to the Circle Sportif with Linda Longbottom and
Nancy Roberson***
Long debates; Greg Moore versus the Jameses' kids over which state was best,
Texas or North Carolina. (We all know who won.)

Recollections Three
Swimming at the Circle Sportif in its many pools
Birthday dates with my dad at the I-House
Shopping dates with my mom the week before going away for school
Steaks at the Peacock. Pizza at the Pizzeria
Friday Fellowships at the Humphries'
Clothes made each summer by "Mr. Pasteur Man"
Building dams in the driveway during the rainy season
Playing Communist and army with the Gayle boys in Tu Duc
Digging a foxhole in the backyard. Covering it with plywood and dirt from the
dig, so no one could tell it was there
Sitting on our VW bus after dark, listening to gunfire and watching the Gatlin
gun tracers race overhead. The very best fireworks display ever!

*Durian *is a rather large fruit prominent in South Vietnam, rather smelly.*
**Plumaria *is* guava.
***The Circle Sportif *was a French sports complex which could be joined for a fee.*

10

School Days, School Days

Laura Kellum Chastain

"Trust in the Lord and do good; live in the land and be safe"
(Psalm 37:3 TEV).

"School days, school days, dear old Golden Rule days." My early school days
were a little different from those of the average American girl. Our trip to
Vietnam by ship took about three weeks. My education was begun on the high
seas, learning ports of call.

My family moved from Da Lat to Nha Trang where I attended a school for
missionaries' children that was located in Nha Trang on the beach. Twelve of
us made up my class that first year. Four in the first grade, 2 in the second,
and 6 in the third. The dorm was at the school, and we often ate our meals
there. For some reason, I remember the beets. We were served beets quite
often. This memory haunts me even today. The children in the dorm were
aged 6 to 12 and their parents were often in dangerous or faraway places. I was
lucky; my parents lived close by.

We were lovingly taught by dedicated Christian teachers. I learned many
lessons that cannot be found in a book. The dedication of those early teachers
played a big role in my becoming a teacher.

When I became a Christian I ran to school to witness to my teachers, classmates, and anyone who would listen. It seemed they had already heard the
good news, so I took off in search of someone else with whom to share. I
decided to tell the street people living in cardboard shacks near our house.

In Vietnam, many of the houses are surrounded by high walls with high
metal gates to admit cars or people. Our home was no different. My plan was
ingenious! I would climb a tree on the edge of the *front cement* (as opposed to
a front yard) and climb high enough to see over the wall. Then I would sing
"Jesus Loves Me" in Vietnamese as loud as I could. I'm not really sure how I
thought this was going to lead them to see their need for Christ, but I saw it
as my ministry. Much later I discovered that I can't carry a tune!

Just before I was to start third grade, my family moved to Cam Ranh. Mom and Dad were not sure what to do about my education. The dorm in Nha Trang was full. A Wycliffe missionary family offered to let me stay with them Monday through Friday each week and go to school. This host family had many children of their own, yet they invited others like me to live with them as well. It was decided. My father would take me to Nha Trang on Monday morning and pick me up on Friday afternoon.

One Monday morning, my dad and I set out for Nha Trang in our usual way. He drove, of course, and I sat in the back singing all the songs I knew. These were mainly church songs and those I learned while practicing piano. Thankfully, he hears about as well as I sing.

This particular day, we had some difficulty getting to school. The Vietcong had blown up several bridges along our route during the night. We had to abandon our car and make our way on foot.

I remember walking single file along the remaining girder of one bridge and leaping to shore. We hitched rides with any vehicle that would carry us, and we didn't reach the school until noon.

I got a lot of mileage out of this adventure with my classmates. I continue to remember it with fondness. I can't recall why we didn't turn back, but we didn't. But then my dad never has turned back when he started something worthwhile.

11

Sister Two

Hope Hayes Hudson

"God is my witness that I tell the truth when I say that my deep feeling
for you all comes from the heart of Christ Jesus himself"
(Phil. 1:8 TEV).

Throughout the years we were in Vietnam we always had a helper. Through a
good portion of those years, the woman I remember most was Chi Hai. She
was magnificently special! Since I was so far away from my grandmothers, Chi
Hai was often their stand-in. She became so much a part of our family that she
moved from Saigon to Can Tho with us. She lived in a room at the back of our
house. I visited with her in her room and we talked—in Vietnamese. When
my parents had to be gone from the house, I stayed with Chi Hai. I felt so safe
with her.

"Sister Two" was an older woman with a neat smile and a nervous little gig-
gle to go with it.* I believe she would have given her life for one of us. We
were her family just as she was ours even though we were cultures apart. My
mouth waters when I think of her foods on our table. This humble woman,
who prepared our meals with elegance and pride, always hoped to please our
family with the work of her hands.

There have not been many times when I have been cooking that I've not said,
"I wish Chi Hai was here!" Because she liked things to be neat and clean, everything was picked up and cleaned the minute you put it down, even if it was not
dirty. So at our house, whenever I do the same, I'm called "little Chi Hai."

I think of her often and wish I knew what has happened to her since our
separation. She had a great influence on my life and I hope and pray she is
alive and well. Memories of her live on in my heart.

*Families in Vietnam often numbered their children as well as named them. Thus, you
have Sister Two, or Four; Brother Two, etc. They always started the numbering with
two, however. So Chi Hai (Sister Two) was really the firstborn girl in the family.

12

Street Without Joy

Diane Davis Casebier

"Show your greatness in the sky, O God, and your glory over
all the earth. Save us by your might; answer my prayer,
so that the people you love may be rescued"
(Psalm 108:5-6 TEV).

I hear the convoy's rumbling roar
That brings the kids to their doors,
To see the Americans and their tanks
The ugly machines from which they shrank.

The GIs' faces sober with deadly grief,
Looking toward war-torn reefs.
I ran out among the grass,
I shyly waved as they thundered past.

Their faces turned, filled with surprise,
And from miles around you could hear their cries.
The names "Grandpa" and "Baby-sitter" and "Gang"
Were colorfully painted on some tanks.
As the soldiers grinned and waved,
Their tanks rolled out into the day . . .
When evening came the roar increasing,
The tanks rolled back through empty streets.

They broke the silence with rumbling—
The sound mounting and doubling,
The men rode through with homebound eyes,
They turned to wave to me good-byes.

Some may have been happy, others grim,
Some for sure had lost a friend.

The war, that war with forever wounds,
The many lives that it doomed.

Those handsome boys with boyish grins,
War has turned to haunted men.

This poem was submitted by Rosalie Beck, who served as a two-year missionary in South Vietnam. She pulled it from her Vietnam memorabilia. Diane wrote it in eighth grade and put this note at the bottom: "This poem is about the American soldiers and tanks that passed my house on Highway 1. This sheet is called 'The Street Without Joy.'"

13

The Blue Beast

Hope Hayes Hudson

"Be joyful always, pray at all times, be thankful in all circumstances. This is
what God wants from you in your life in union with Christ Jesus"
(1 Thess. 5:16-18 TEV).

The "Blue Beast" was an old Volkswagen van that the MKs (missionaries' kids)
hated to ride in. It would invariably break down. It was just *old*. The MKs
named it the "Blue Beast" because of its color.

The Blue Beast
Rickety, rackety, here I come . . .
to school I will take
the MK bunch from Saigon across
the city to Cholon's streets I will . . .
I will go . . . go . . . go . . .
Rickety, rackety, here I come . . .

"The Blue Beast" is my name
so affectionately called, I have
done my daily duty, and under
skilled hand of chauffeur I go
to rest for tomorrow's show
on the road.

Thank you, thank you,
"Blue Beast," for the days you
let me ride to school in you.
You were part of memories
I hold close to my heart.
There were days we'd

pray you would not start!
But you came through
to the bitter end—
Thank you, "*Blue Beast*,"
my dear old friend.

Transportation was hard to come by in Vietnam. Bicycles, motorcycles, the vans that always had to be pushed—and worked on; and the old French Citröen that the Myerses drove in Da Nang, that wouldn't go in reverse! "Transportation Share" had to be put in place when there weren't enough vehicles to go around. In later years, we tried ordering cars from neighboring countries—they were cheaper but sometimes required a little rebuilding. The little Mazdas that ran without being pushed or cajoled into performing were hoorayed and petted like Cadillacs when they first rolled off a ship toward one of our homes.

14

The Freight

Diane Davis Casebier

"You have been raised to life with Christ, so set your hearts on the things
that are in heaven, . . . not on things here on earth"
(Col. 3:1-2 TEV).

The freight came filled with furlough treats,
Of packaged cakes that taste not sweet,
But of flakes sifted from detergent soap.

A box of toys for each kid,
From stateside stores,
A private hoard.
Of pecans in brown bags,
That had aged and smelled
Like fall in Texas Piney Woods.

Of bikes we bought
Of shoes to grow into
With pre-scuffed soles to pass customs.
Of great smelling deodorants and shampoos,
Enough to last for four years use.

Returning boxes of "missionary wares"
That were shown church to church of our "home,"
That looked out of place among the spoils
"Of a furloughing year in our private 'Disneyland.'"

Letters and packages from family and churches were like Christmas lights. The packages brought smiles, shouts, grins, or sometimes—the droops—if contents had been pilfered, or weren't the fulfillment of "the visions of sugarplums dancing in our heads."

15

The Sandy Alleyway

Katherine Compher Cocks

"Dear friends, let us love one another, because love comes from God.
Whoever loves is a child of God and knows God"
(1 John 4:7 TEV).

Children at times experience traumatic losses such as the death of a loved one, divorce of their parents, etc. For me it was leaving Vietnam at the age of 11. Though my missionary parents were American, I had come to think, act, and feel more like a Vietnamese—I had moved there at the age of 2 months. I spoke fluent Vietnamese, dreamed in Vietnamese, played dolls in Vietnamese, and my closest friends were Vietnamese. But as I look back to my childhood in Vietnam, all I have left are my memories and images of a country now closed to most of the outside world.

Most of my memories reside in Qui Nhon, a coastal city in the middle of Vietnam. I was 5 years old when we arrived in Qui Nhon; I had spent the first 4 years of my life in other parts of the country. Dad drove my family in a white station wagon down a sandy alleyway near the end of a row of Chinese-style row houses to our new home. The whole neighborhood came out to stare at this White American family moving into their alleyway. I peered anxiously from the car windows wondering if I would find friends here. After moving in and settling down, Thuy became my best friend. Her father held a high position in the local government, and he assisted my dad when able.

Though I had an array of American store-bought toys, I shunned them to create games with my new friends in the sandy alleyway. We used rocks as playing pieces on gameboards we drew in the sand. We drew elaborate hopscotch designs in the sand—each more difficult to accomplish than the previous ones. We made Chinese jump ropes out of hundreds of rubber bands woven together intricately, anchored between our big silly toes, and then we performed various feats with them. And if we fell, the sand cushioned our fall. When we were hungry, we tied sticks together with rubber bands and used them to knock the fruit and berries off the neighbor's trees. We would then scamper in the sand, each trying to gather the most fruit for herself.

As much as the Vietnamese influenced my life, I influenced theirs. At my house my friends found out what a Western bathroom looked like. A Vietnamese toilet was a hole in a concrete base that they would squat over. Mom, trying to keep life normal for me invited friends over for American-style special occasion parties. Such games as pin-the-tail-on-the-donkey, pop the balloon, and bob for apples (using guavas as substitutes) were learned and enjoyed. I remember one year I received a battery-operated walking doll Mom had ordered by mail. Thuy liked it so much that Mom and Dad ordered her one. But to her parents it was such a fancy toy, they displayed it in a showcase.

Most Americans have memories of celebrating Christmas or Thanksgiving. For me, the Vietnamese had two holidays that will always remain special. The first was a fall harvest celebration. The children made or brought lanterns of papier-mâché, cellophane, or cardboard. At night we placed a lighted candle in the middle of our lanterns. Everyone marched around the alleyway displaying their handiwork. It was quite a feat to make it through the night without one's lantern burning up.

The other celebration was the Chinese New Year, referred to as Tet. Several days before Tet, neighbors made hundreds of rice cakes, wrapped them in banana leaves, and steamed them all night in a burning caldron. These were served during the holidays as relatives and friends came to visit. I always went over to Thuy's house because visitors would give red envelopes of money to all the children in the household. I usually came out with a fistful of those little envelopes.

A pastime for Vietnamese women was to pick lice out of each other's hair, squash the lice, and do all of this while catching up on the gossip. Much to Mom's dismay, I felt really accepted when I got my first case of lice and ran over to the neighbor's house to have them pull lice from my hair. Mom quickly ordered numerous tubes of antilice shampoo and made me and all my friends use it. But a greater medical problem was getting rid of intestinal parasites. I often escaped Mom's watchful eye and bought food sold by the itinerant food vendors. I remember frequent doses of deworming medicines.

Right after my 11th birthday the North Vietnamese prepared for another offensive campaign. We were told by the American consulate to leave our town. As my family and I drove away from that sandy alleyway, I again peered out the car window, nervous and sad. I knew that the friends and neighbors who stared at us this time probably would never be seen by us again. I fought to hold back the tears, and inside I begged God to find a way to let me stay and live at the house on the sandy alleyway with my friends.

To this day I cannot watch a movie or TV show about Vietnam without crying—sometimes for days. But for as long as I live, I will retain the richness brought to my life from living in Vietnam.

16

They're Not Shooting at Us

Diane Davis Casebier

"I trust in the Lord for safety. How foolish of you to say to me,
'Fly away like a bird to the mountains, because the wicked have drawn their
bows and aimed their arrows to shoot from the shadows at good men'"
(Psalm 11:1-2 TEV).

Always the innocent pay during war . . .
They're not shooting at us
But you can't play out at night.
They're not shooting at us
But there are mines barbed down the lane.
They're not shooting at us
Put your head under the bed.
They're not shooting at us
But in case they miss . . .
They're not shooting at us
But close your shutters and don't turn on the light.
They're not shooting at us
Come down to the patio—we're hid—for a bite.
They're not shooting at us
But Dad has pulled the van to block our play area from the street.
They're not shooting at us
But be sure to lock your outside door when you sleep.
They're not shooting at us
But board the plane, we've got to leave.
They're not shooting at us
Good-bye to cat and dog plus years of stuff.
They're not shooting at us
But Dad stayed behind as we left.
They're not shooting at us

Pack your bag in case this time.
They're not shooting at us
We flee again by Counsel's advice.
They're not shooting at us
But Mom's with us in Taiwan.
Dad—we didn't know—boarded a refugee barge
Ended up in the Philippines . . .
They're not shooting at us.

17

Together

Hope Hayes Hudson

"You are always in my heart!"
(Phil. 1:7a TEV).

All of the MKs (missionaries' kids) really looked forward to times together!
Once a year all the missionaries got together for the annual meetings or
retreats, perhaps in Da Lat or Vung Tau, where we'd have loads of fun with
each other and our teachers—sort of a Vacation Bible School, only more fun!
I would get to see my very best girlfriends in the world, Deborah and Diane
Davis, Margaret Myers, and Deborah James. Those times we spent together
were unlike any other. We spent time playing, going to the market to shop,
and trying to outbargain each other with the shopkeepers. Of course we would
also tease each other about our secret boyfriends and spy on the older MKs.
In our serious moments we shared our love for God and Vietnam.

When the time came to return home, we would all cry, realizing that it
would be another year before we would be together again. We were all part of
the same family! The Vietnam family, the Mission family, and the family of God.

The War

1

A Holiday Explodes

Priscilla Compher

"He sets the time for love and the time for hate, the time for war
and the time for peace"
(Eccl. 3:8 TEV).

Our most trying experience during our first term of missionary service? The answer requires no thought: the Tet offensive of 1968.

We had stayed up on the eve of Tet to watch the fireworks. Sleep was impossible anyway. The government declared fireworks legal for the festive celebration this year. People bought and bought. Early in the evening firecrackers released their fury, and rockets headed for the skies. By midnight the city sky was bright with massive and ornate explosions of light and sound.

Two American servicemen were our guests. As we watched the sky, they kept commenting that some of the explosions looked like shots from a familiar gun. About 1:00 A.M. we drove the servicemen back to their villa. We went to bed.

Later that morning, Bob left for an early church service near the center of town; a bout with intestinal flu kept me home. Casually, I turned on the radio to practice hearing the Vietnamese language. The Vietnamese I heard, however, reported heavy fighting going on in most major cities of Vietnam, including Nha Trang where we lived. Fighting was going on in the center of town and in the suburbs where our church at Phuoc Hai was located. The servicemen were right. The attack had started during the festivities, camouflaged successfully under the blanket of joy.

Within a few minutes, Bob returned. The service was canceled due to what appeared to be heavy fighting near the military compounds. Shortly after his return, high school students from the church in Phuoc Hai appeared. The fighting was close to the church, they said. Fearful they would be captured by the Vietcong and forced to fight for them, they asked for refuge.

For several days we stayed in our house; sometimes we slept at a servicemen's center where the American military provided armed protection. While staying inside, we explored different avenues of entertaining the housebound children. The American military had recently introduced television into Vietnam with military-scheduled programming. For several days and nights, while the beginning of the end of South Vietnam was being launched nearby with the Vietcong Tet offensive of 1968, our children sat in the living room, with their eyes glued to a World War II-based combat series.

2

A Mom's Prayer

Betty J. Merrell

"My God will supply all your needs"
(Phil. 4:19b TEV).

Spring 1968, Da Nang. The big Tet offensive was rocking, raping, and battering the cities of South Vietnam. US Marines encircled Da Nang like a fortress wall. Rockets hit Da Nang nightly. One night they came so close to our house on the bay that our locked doors opened. The earthquake-jarred doors that opened wide during Paul's jail experience in Philippi came alive to me that night.

On such nights Ron and I held each other close, our eyes opened wide in the black of the uncertain night. "Maybe we should go home tomorrow," we would whisper. But as we watched the magnificent sunrise over the South China Sea bay each morning, it seemed foolish to leave. Was it not an intervention of God during those days that our two young sons slept right through every night?

All but one letter from friends and relatives in the US brought a concerned demand: "Get out—leave. Hurry." Then one letter arrived amid the "get-out" letters. I recognized the handwriting of my mother and saved it for the last reading. She wrote, "Dear Sis, The news is bad there? It sounds like it from here. I am praying, however, that you can stay there to do what the Lord has called you there to do."

How blessed I was to receive the settling-down and settling-in prayer of a godly mother. I knew that every morning she knelt by a certain chair in the living room and talked with her Lord Jesus about her daughter in Vietnam. She also prayed for her other daughter in Tulsa, her son in Arizona, and a number of other folks she met in her daily walks in and out of the houses of Red Fork, a suburban area of Tulsa, Oklahoma. I am confident that God listened to my mother's intimate prayers and guided us through some traumatic days that followed the day we received her letter.

3

Curfew's Toll

Rosalie Beck

"Let God's people rejoice in their triumph and sing joyfully all night long"
(Psalm 149:5 TEV).

When I first arrived in Vietnam, I watched wide-eyed as my Cathay Airlines
jet taxied past bunkers, fighter jets, and antiaircraft artillery pieces. Finally it
came to a halt at the international entry building. The jet was surrounded by
soldiers with automatic weapons. I thought, *I'll never get used to this.* But I did.
When war is part of your life daily, you become accustomed to its inconve-
niences—but never to its cruelty or insanity—or to its dark humor.

In Da Lat where I worked with the youth in two churches, Wednesday
night was special. It was prayer meeting night. The missionaries, and sometimes other westerners, gathered at the home of Earl and Sherry Bengs for
prayer and Bible study. Then they petitioned the Lord together. It was a sweet
and special two hours for us all. Sometimes it was the only period all week in
which I heard and spoke English.

After prayers, we always ate dessert.

One evening Sherry, Beth Goad, Barbara Lassiter, and I were making
sopapillas for the group. Sherry fried the batter and handed them to us for the
sugaring. As she worked in her kitchen, she expressed concern for her sister's
safety. Sherry had just received a letter from her sister who was driving from
Florida to New Orleans to visit their parents. Sherry worried that in order to
keep that timetable, her sister would have to travel after curfew!

I had just put a pastry in my mouth and almost choked. Beth and Barbara
looked at one another. Beth gently said to Sherry, "Sherry, they don't have curfew in America." Sherry had become accustomed to managing her life by the
curfew sirens at 6:00 A.M. and 11:00 P.M. The first freed her to leave the house
and the second warned her not to leave. It was so second-nature to live by curfew that Sherry now thought as though the entire world lived by the siren's
wailing directions. One does become accustomed to the ways of war.

4

In Harm's Way

Priscilla Compher

"The Lord is my shepherd; I have everything I need. He lets me rest in fields of green grass and leads me to quiet pools of fresh water" (Psalm 23:1-2 TEV).

We tried to shield our children from the realities of the war whenever possible. When bodies of the dead were on display for whatever reason, we refrained from going by there. When bodies lay strewn along a highway, we told Douglas, David, and Cathy to get down on the floor of the car. We traveled from our area by car very few times.

During one seemingly peaceful period, we drove to Da Lat up in the mountains for our annual Mission retreat. The scenery was beautiful, and all was calm. On our return to Qui Nhon, we talked about it and decided we would travel by car more frequently to the major city south of us for fellowship with another missionary family who had three sons about the ages of our boys.

While we were discussing that, we followed the curve of a mountain pass. As we rounded the curve, we noticed a large truck had gone over the ridge. Men were hauling items out of the truck. Suddenly, it hit us—an ambush. Shots rang out and dirt came flying through the air. Merciful heavens, were *we* being shot at? The children and I ducked down and Bob lowered his head as much as possible while pumping the gas pedal with all the stamina his foot could muster. We sped away out of gunfire range. God spared us from physical harm. Many months passed before we considered another trip by car.

One night we were awakened by successive deafening explosions. Concussions were so strong that our locked doors were opened. Some doors came off their hinges, and window panes shattered. Later, we learned that a military ammunition dump had caught fire. Although the ordnance dump was a number of miles away and a mountain separated our city from the dump, damage occurred to the tile-roofed houses in Qui Nhon.

Rather frequently, mortars or rockets were shot at military installations near or in Qui Nhon. Most of the time we were not in serious danger. American servicemen taught in our English classes. Bob would pick them up in the late afternoon and drive them back to their barracks about 10:00 P.M. Occasionally, Bob would get caught at an American installation when it was under attack.

By far, the most dangerous period of time for our family during our second term was during the spring offensive of 1972. The northern third of our province had been overrun by the Communist forces. Heavy fighting was now centered in the middle portion of the province. We lived in the southern part of Binh Dinh and were receiving some mortar and rocket attacks.

One day exactly at noon, the elementary school across from our sandy road sent the children home. Bob took one of the twins to check on the progress of the church construction project. They had just pulled away from the house when they heard the whiz of a rocket going over the house. It exploded in the road at the main entrance of the elementary school. The two children at home, our helper, and I ran to an inside room, our designated shelter when we sensed danger. Once there I thought about our missing two family members. Just as I was thinking they might have been killed, they scrambled in the front door.

What saved them? On that day, hundreds of schoolchildren elected to take the side door of the school as their exit into the narrow alley that led to the main road. The press of that crowd had blockaded any forward movement of our car onto that main road. Our family was intact; some schoolchildren not at the side entrance were killed; others were wounded. Shopkeepers across from the school were injured or dead.

The incident traumatized our children. Their faces went white with fear. Mortars and rockets fell that day again at 2:00 P.M. People had decided the noon attack was over, they could return to school, or go to the market. The main market was hit.

For several weeks we had watched people pack up and flee south. Eventually, 80 percent of the people in Binh Dinh took to the roads. Our vacation to Singapore was one month away. We decided to move our plans ahead to give our family some relief from danger and from the *fear* of danger.

It was impossible at such a time to get reservations on the commercial airlines of Air Vietnam. They were booked and packed. We packed our bags and Bob drove us to the former American airfield, now a Vietnamese installation as most American military forces had been pulled out. Bob dropped us off and he returned to the house to leave the car. He walked back to the airfield to wait with us.

We had heard that an American C-130 cargo plane would be landing to pick up a forklift for return to Saigon for safekeeping. We hoped we could catch a ride. Rather like hitchhiking along the runway! But waiting along with us were American military personnel who were stranded in Qui Nhon earlier in the day when their plane developed engine trouble. They did not want to stay in Qui Nhon overnight. About 100 Vietnamese civilians were waiting, too.

In late afternoon, the plane landed and Bob approached the pilots. The American servicemen did likewise. Along with them and the forklift, we flew out of Qui Nhon into Saigon where we boarded a commercial flight for Singapore and a much-needed respite from the rigors of raging onslaught.

5

Jogging in a Minefield

Rosalie Beck

"He promised to rescue us from our enemies and allow us to serve
him without fear, so that we might be holy and righteous before
him all the days of our life"
(Luke 1:74-75 TEV).

The Vietnam journeyman's (two-year missionary) ability to adapt to situations
was tested at a retreat at Hue in 1974. The Vietnam Baptist Mission understood about journeymen. From arrival until departure, missionaries made
every effort to help each journeyman learn everything possible about the work
in the country. As a result, journeymen sometimes saw more of the nation
than the missionaries in their assigned locations did. Twice each year we spent
a weekend at one of the Mission stations. The host missionaries there showed
us their work and taught us how to pray intelligently for their specific needs.
Being a journeyman in Vietnam gave me the opportunity to travel across the
countryside and see its mountains, beaches, jungles, and rural villages. But
because the country was Vietnam in the 1960s and 1970s, everything carried
the stain of war.

Hue, the old imperial capital, suffered greatly in the Tet offensive. Many of
the ancient and treasured buildings were destroyed or damaged. Even so, it
was an imposing city. Linda Pegram, Doug Kellum, Phyllis Tyler, Andy Wright,
Greg Holden, and I gathered for our weekend in Hue under the supervision of
Bob and Ida Davis, the resident missionaries. Bob arranged for our visit to the
city of Quang Tri.

The Vietnamese called Quang Tri their Hiroshima because it was the only
major city destroyed by the war. Squatting on the river that separated North
and South Vietnam, Quang Tri was important to both sides. When the
Northern and Southern Vietnamese fought over it, every building was
destroyed.

The morning of our journey, we climbed into a Mission van and headed toward the demilitarized zone. At the entry checkpoint, the guard told Bob our papers were not valid and we'd have to get other papers. After trying for a couple of hours to get the papers, Bob decided to take a shortcut around the checkpoint into the zone. The van was soon stuck in a huge sand drift. Though Mission vans were great for transporting groups of people, they lacked power to pull out of a sand drift. We pushed, we pulled, we dug, we did everything we could with no success. The guys were discussing what to do next when one of the MKs (missionaries' kids) with us, Grey Myers, noticed a large pile of howitzer shell casings nearby. We flattened one end of the 1½-foot-long brass casings and jammed it under the van's back tires. The van shuddered and pulled free of the sand. A battle fought at this site two years earlier had provided our way out of the sand trap.

As we climbed back into the van, Greg looked at Andy and suggested they should jog in front of the car checking for land mines. Since the road ran through a war zone, it probably had been mined. It seems crazy that two men would check out a road by such a method and at such risk. But at that time, Andy and Greg's actions were dictated quite naturally by the world in which we functioned.

Greg and Andy found no mines and we eventually made it into the demilitarized zone. Across the river, I watched two North Vietnamese swimming on their sides. I thought, *How strange my life is at this moment. With war as the norm, ordinary people view the most bizarre behavior as normal and rational.*

6
Letter to Grandmas: Unsent

Betty J. Merrell

"Though war rise up against me, yet I will be confident"
(Psalm 27:3*b* NRSV).

Tim, aged four, was dictating a letter to his two grandmas. We usually sent the same letter to both grandmothers. I typed along as he spoke slowly.

Dear Grandma,
I know you hear lots of things about Vietnam on the radio or read them in the papers. You probably think it's real bad here, but it isn't. It's pretty nice here. Our living room is all sandbagged.

Love,
Tim

PS This is a letter the mother didn't send until long after that crisis was over. I judged that *sandbags* might be a little too much for two grandmothers to digest.

7

Michael's Birth

Rachel James

"The angel wearing linen clothes said, 'At that time the great
angel Michael, who guards your people, will appear'"
(Dan. 12:1*a* TEV).

We were living 12 kilometers north of Saigon in the little village of Thu Duc
in February 1968, when the now infamous and terribly destructive
Communist offensive called the Tet offensive began. For five days we could
not leave our house until the "friendly forces" brought a measure of security
to the village. During these five days, we had no electricity or water. The road
into the city of Saigon was often blocked by war actions. A strictly enforced
curfew was put in place throughout the area beginning each evening at 9:00
P.M. Any vehicle caught on the road after that hour ran great risk of being shot.
I was five months pregnant.

I often agonized about what I would do if I should suddenly go into labor
during the night curfew. Fighting on the main road into Saigon, even during
the day, made travel into the city uncertain. Following the Tet offensive, our
missionary women and children in the southern area of Vietnam decided to
evacuate to Bangkok, Thailand, until the situation stabilized.

Six missionary wives and their children arrived in Bangkok on February
16, about two weeks after the offensive began. Our families were scattered in
apartments in the same general area of Bangkok. We were relieved to learn
that our husbands could visit once every six weeks during our stay in
Bangkok. They timed their visits so that one of them would be in Thailand
every week to bring news from Vietnam.

We immediately made a decision to meet together weekly for prayer and
fellowship as was our missionary custom in Vietnam. As the months passed, I
realized that the Mission in Thailand would be meeting on June 10, the date
our baby was due. The meeting was scheduled for Pattaya, on the coast of
Thailand far south of the city of Bangkok. That meant that none of the

Thailand missionaries would be in the city to help with my three small children while I was in the hospital. The Vietnam Mission was meeting the same week in Da Nang on the coast of Vietnam. All Vietnam missionary women and children were making preparation to return to Vietnam prior to that meeting. Here I was in the huge, crowded city of Bangkok with three small children, expecting a fourth, speaking no Thai language, and with no fellow missionaries in the city during the time of the birth of my baby.

I was asked to share a devotional thought at our weekly prayer meeting. I knew what I wanted to say, and I was trying to find a Scripture verse to fit my thoughts. During my search, a quiet peace came over me. I did not know how God would work out the details which were troubling me, but I just came to the realization that He would work them out.

On May 29 my husband, Sam, was on the coast of Vietnam at Cam Ranh attending a trustee meeting for a new orphanage. During the early hours of the meeting he became very restless and was overwhelmed by a desire to leave for Thailand. Through a series of miracles he left Cam Ranh early in the morning, arrived in Saigon at noon, and departed for Bangkok in the late afternoon. At eight o'clock in the evening on May 29 he arrived at our apartment in Bangkok. Unknown to him I had a doctor's appointment scheduled for the next morning.

At 11:00 A.M. I arrived as scheduled at the doctor's office in the Seventh Day Adventist Hospital. I asked him, "Have you ever delivered a baby 'by appointment'?" He replied, "It depends on how ready you are." He admitted me into the hospital at 1:00 P.M. and immediately started to induce labor. At 3:00 P.M. our fourth baby, a boy, was born. The date was May 30, a full ten days before he was due. Once that boy was born, the doctor told me that he was due to leave on vacation the following day and had intended to place me in the care of another doctor whom I had never met. Once again God had marvelously intervened to work out all the details about which I had been so anxious.

In searching for a name for our baby we became aware that Michael, the archangel in the Old Testament, was present in a miraculous way with Israel in one of her darkest hours. We realized that our baby was born during one of those dark hours in our family's life. God had been present in a miraculous way with us. We named him Michael.

Sam was present in Bangkok to stay with the children during the time I was hospitalized. When I returned to our apartment from the hospital, he returned to Vietnam to be present for the Mission's annual meeting on June 10. Six weeks later I, the three children I had brought to Bangkok, *and* Michael returned to Vietnam where we reunited with Sam as a family.

8

One Woman's Seasons

Beth Goad

"God's plan is to make known his secret to his people, this rich and glorious secret which he has for all peoples. And the secret is that Christ is in you, which means that you will share in the glory of God. So we preach Christ to everyone. With all possible wisdom we warn and teach them in order to bring each one into God's presence as a mature individual in union with Christ" (Col. 1:27-28 TEV).

Vietnam was not a place of happy endings. Our family arrived in the country in 1973. A cease-fire had been agreed upon. Everyone hoped for peace. Yet every day brought more deaths in the incessant fighting. On the days the country's plight seemed without hope, those who were believers looked to Christ and saw hope. Mrs. Suc was one of them.

I remember it well: 1974, four days before Easter in Da Lat, Vietnam's mountain resort town. I looked up from the test at the language school and into the eyes of Mrs. Suc on the porch. Now Mrs. Suc should have been at the home of Bob and Ginnie Tripp—caring for their two sons. The Tripps, serving with the Assembly of God Mission, began language school when we did in July 1973. Mrs. Suc was their helper. *Perhaps one of the Tripps's sons is ill,* I thought, and returned to the test. At that moment Ginnie Tripp burst into the classroom crying, "Mr. Suc has been electrocuted!"

Our concern for the Suc family was great. We had been there when Mrs. Suc walked into the baptismal waters shortly after Christmas 1973. We were there the next year when two of her seven children were baptized on Palm Sunday 1974. Mr. Suc was a soldier, an electrician for the military. Now 30,000 volts of electricity had passed through the upper part of his body. Mrs. Suc was told her husband was dead; she headed for the hospital, but she did not find a dead husband. She found an alive husband. That night the doctor amputated his left arm into the shoulder.

Our hearts were heavy that evening. We made our way to our regular

Wednesday prayer meeting with other missionaries. Earl Bengs, resident missionary in Da Lat, had returned to the hospital to be with the family during the surgery. Most of our praying that evening was intercession for this family and for Earl, that he might be God's instrument of comfort and strength.

Thursday morning Mr. Suc was still alive! He was conscious, alert, and wanted to talk with *the missionary*. Earl spoke softly with his deep voice: "Miraculously, the Lord has given you yet another opportunity to hear and believe the gospel." His interest was visible. He indicated an awareness that God had indeed spared him.

Doctors, however, were offering no medical hope—Suc "might live four days at most," they forecast. "Internal damage likely has been sustained: kidneys and lungs are functioning far below normal." They decided to fly him to the military hospital in Saigon, where better equipment was available.

Suc survived the flight to Saigon. We praised the Lord. Days dragged into weeks; at every word of improvement we thanked God.

The community where the Suc family lived was astir. They knew that Mrs. Suc and two of her children had chosen to follow the new religion. But why had Americans sat with the family during the long hours at the hospital? Why was Suc still alive? He should be dead with all he had endured. Yet they saw him alive and gaining strength daily! They must have thought: *Only a God of tremendous power could do that!* They asked to know more about Him. The Lord stirred many of those hearts.

Several weeks later in Da Lat, Mrs. Suc received the dreaded word. Her husband had died. She and her children made the long, sorrowful trip to Saigon. When they arrived, they found that the message had been a mistake! Suc was still very much alive and improving.

But a day without joy followed. Another message arrived, this time not in error. Suc had lost his balance on the bed, and having only one arm to support himself as he turned, he fell to the floor and to his death. Our hearts ached and ached for his wife and those children. No happy ending to the story after all.

But the widow's faith hung strong. When some of her Buddhist neighbors came bringing various articles to ward off evil spirits, she allowed them to be placed in her house. Later she removed them. "They do not go with my following the way of Christ," she explained.

During the same week of her husband's death, Mrs. Suc received word that a brother-in-law had been killed in a delta fray. She sent her oldest child, a daughter studying in Saigon, to bring his body home for burial. As the daughter was returning to Saigon, mortar fire hit the vehicle in which she was riding, and she was killed. Some time later, Mrs. Suc's older brother was killed in fighting near Da Nang.

Our human impulse was to shout, "Why, Lord, must this happen to this dear new child of Yours?" We had no answers; but we had something better than answers. We offered her the truths of God's promises and the adequacy of His special grace. We taught her: He enables us to praise Him even in grief.

For those without Christ, the future outlook in Vietnam was black indeed. I heard Vietnamese believers say, "I look at my homeland and despair that we will ever know peace. Yet in my despair, I remember to look to Christ—and I pray."

Christ was the hope to so few of those in despair. For so many others, no one told them about promises and grace for the real-life stuff of nonhappy endings.

Practicing Luke, Chapter Three

Betty J. Merrell

"Whoever has two shirts must give one to the man who has none"
(Luke 3:11a TEV).

Every night my two sons and I would climb onto the bed with a Bible and another book. I had brought a four-year supply of books to Vietnam for our first term. We read every night: One chapter or story in the Bible and one chapter in the other book. The night before this story we had visited John the Baptist and Winnie the Pooh.

Now you should also know that the first refugees to come into Baptist purview in Da Lat had moved into a garagelike building sitting on the back of the lot that housed the language center. Like Joseph and Mary, they had appeared one day with no "crib for their beds," nor money for a room in the inn. Missionaries in Da Lat scurried around and made a room in the inn out of the building in the back by scrounging from one another or buying the necessities to place therein.

I came home from language classes one day (home was next door) and found Chi Ba agitated, or as close to it as she would ever get—for she was of gentle spirit.

"Oh, Madam," she whispered, "little Danny has taken all his toys to the little boy in the family next door."

Now, toys came from limited sources for MKs (missionaries' kids) in Vietnam. You shipped them along with your furniture when you came, people sent them as gifts, or you made them. A few Vietnamese toys could be bought at market.

I found Danny, who was five. "Tell me about your day," I asked. He spoke excitedly. "You know in the story last night, John the Baptist told the people that if they had two bowls of soup and someone else didn't have any, the one who had two should give one to the other boy. And if one boy had two coats and . . . ." I let him finish telling me the story. Well, that was pretty close, I reflected.

I may be stuck here, I thought. I told the story, I believed the teaching—giving out of our abundance to those experiencing a lack. I could not contradict that. I dared not contradict it. I knew he couldn't think ahead to the consequences of his action, so Mama did it for him—not out loud, of course. I knew this child would soon discover that John's big truth and Danny's extreme practice of it meant all his own playthings were gone.

I gently approached John's formula—now Dan's. "Why don't we just go see your new friend and his mom?" I suggested. As we walked in, I noted everything was tidy—a home had appeared where an old building once was. We two moms passed congenialities of the day, until a conversational door opened that introduced the toy experience. I shared with her the story from "God's Holy Book" that we'd read together the night before. She was visibly moved by it.

"Well," I grinned, "Danny went even further than John," I noted. "He gave away *all* his toys." Then it hit her. "Oh, my, now Hiep must practice the story," she said. She called Danny's new friend in and told him the story. "Now, Danny has no toys, and you have all of them," she said, a little sadly. *Sometimes mamas are so smart,* I thought. *I bet they're like that all over the world.*

Hiep called Danny over, and spread the toys out. The two picked and chose and picked and chose until all the toys were sorted by their mutually agreed-upon process: "I'll take this one," "I want that one."

Until that moment, the new kid on the block didn't have a clue about John the Baptist. He barely had one about Danny. Danny had arrived in Da Lat not too long before Hiep had. Hiep spoke no English, and Danny was just beginning to initiate his tongue to conversational Vietnamese with Chi Ba in the kitchen behind the house. But both boys had trounced around in the wilderness with John the Baptist in Luke, chapter 3 that day, and then they turned around and preached his sermon for us in living color.

I've often wondered what I would have done if Hiep's mom hadn't caught that teaching moment. Could I have walked away from *all* those toys? I wonder. That was one of the days a son taught his mother the lesson. It's happened a lot of times since then.

10

The Man in Black

Celia Moore

"My enemies will know the bitter shame of defeat; in sudden
confusion they will be driven away"
(Psalm 6:10 TEV).

Our peaceful lunch was suddenly interrupted by a voice saying in broken
English, "I am a Vietcong. Your house is surrounded, any show of force will
result in your death." The .38 caliber revolver at my husband's head didn't
move. He opened his black jacket to reveal four hand grenades wired together and taped to his body. He continued in his broken English, "Any attempt of
retaliation will result in the detonation of the grenades, destroying everyone
in this room."

Those in the room included missionary journeyman, Lee Weems; my husband, Peyton; and me. Lee and I had just returned from the Baptist
Communication Center. Peyton, who was director of the center, was recuperating from a back injury and could only move around on crutches. While eating, we had been discussing the morning's activities, the response to the cor-
respondence courses, progress in recording radio programs, the translation of
movie scripts, etc.

What did he want? Well, anything portable and of value. He pilfered for
any American or Vietnamese currency, jewelry, cameras, etc. Suddenly, he
lurched toward me. He ordered Peyton out of the bed and led the two men at
gunpoint to a nearby bathroom. He locked the door.

Just as he returned to the bedroom, the telephone rang. He led me down
the stairs and ordered me to answer. The caller was a missionary coordinating
hospitality for a family returning from furlough. Would it be possible for us to
have the family for lunch the next day? Customarily we were delighted to provide hospitality and fellowship for any missionary family or GI. What could I
say that would give some warning of the danger we were facing? "Barbara," I
said, "I can't be bothered with that right now." I deliberately tried to sound

abrupt and rude. But, Barbara knew me well enough to know that this was not my usual reaction. She inquired if something was wrong, to which I answered, "Yes." "We'll be over as soon as we can," she said.

The man in black led me back to the bedroom. He ordered me to get on the bed. As nervous as I was, I suddenly felt an uncanny calm and peace come over me. I now know it to be the power of the prayers of the men in the room nearby. Amazingly, the Lord gave me the ability to witness to this man in his own language. I shared with him our purpose for being in Vietnam. I told him of Jesus' love for him and his people.

At the mention of Jesus' name he became enraged and yelled at me to "shut up." Then, a strange thing happened. It was as if a glass wall came between us. He could not touch me. His eyes held a look of resignation and disgust. He ordered me to give him my engagement and wedding rings and an heirloom ring. I begged him to let me keep a watch which belonged to my deceased mother. I knew the strong Vietnamese reverence for ancestors. Much to my surprise he actually allowed me to keep the watch.

He then marched me to the room where the men were imprisoned. Again, he locked the door. All three were greatly relieved that no one had been injured or molested. After what seemed like an eternity, we heard the shouts of our helper. She had been struck on the head with a gun barrel and threatened with murder if she raised an alarm. She unlocked the door and we were freed.

A few moments later our little daughter returned from school. We thanked God that she was spared the trauma and danger of what had just happened. As we knelt to praise and thank God for His watchcare, tears of joy flowed down our cheeks.

As I often look at my mother's watch, I am reminded of the man in black and the millions like him who do not know Jesus. The command is still, "Go ye" and the promise is still, "Lo, I am with you always, even unto the end of the world."

The trauma of this experience drove a question into the minds of Peyton and Celia Moore. Should they, could they stay in Vietnam? On a Sunday morning several weeks later, they moved to the front of Trinity Baptist Church, Peyton to the piano, Celia to the podium. "This song is the answer we have reached," Peyton said. He started to move his fingers over the keys, slowly, deliberately—Celia opened her mouth, "Sweet little Jesus boy, they made you be bawn in a manguh. Sweet little holy child, they didn't know who you wuz. 'De worl' treat you mean, Lord; dey treat me mean, too. But dat's how things is down heah, dey don't know who you is."

The Moores remained in Vietnam until the forced exodus of 1975.

11

The Protest

Betty J. Merrell

"As for us, we have this large crowd of witnesses around us"
(Heb. 12:1*a* TEV).

With our husbands away on a survey trip to the city of Hue, Celia Moore and I loaded our four boys and one girl into the Volkswagen van and drove toward the marketplace and shops of Da Lat.

As we approached the business area, we noted an unusually large crowd of people. Suddenly, the Volkswagen motor died, with us in it, of course, in the middle of the street. Now that wasn't anything unusual, but in the few months we'd been in Da Lat studying the language, Celia and I had done little driving of the vans, so there we were.

The policeman on duty came to the window. "Move the car," he ordered. "A parade is scheduled in a moment and you've got to get this car out of the way." In our inept Vietnamese, we tried to answer him. "We'd like to move it, but we can't get it started." This dialogue was repeated several times.

Suddenly the parade started! To our surprise, the parade wasn't a parade at all—not from our perspective. We would label it a protest, a demonstration. The first marchers carried flags, the second held a huge banner. "Oh, my goodness. Look at that," Celia and I said at the same time to one another. The words on the lead banner led to a quick action. We decided we'd be less conspicuous out of the car. We asked some men to help us push the car over enough to let traffic pass. Once pushed, we took the children and stood over against a building. The lead banner read, "**Americans, Go Home**!" and other banners shouted derivatives of that. And there we stood. We never looked so American.

Then a voice called out, "Mrs. Moore, Mrs. Merrell!" We slyly looked around to find the voice. Afraid to look, but too curious not to look. When we found its source, it led us straight to Binh, one of our English language students—and he was carrying the lead banner. I had a momentary flash of Ron coming back to town to find wife and children embarking on a Vietnam fishing boat—exiled. But Binh was beaming and waving with enthusiasm—obviously making no connection to the sign he was carrying and the two American women he was greeting so profusely. Whatever sliver of hope we had that we could blend into the wall incognito slid right out of sight when our names were called out with such volume and gusto.

Actually, no one else seemed to get as excited about us as Binh did. The parade was soon over. A helpful gentleman offered to help us start the car, and the day progressed from that challenge to another.

Not one of the three of us ever mentioned the incident until one day months later when Binh had become sad and disillusioned. He returned to Da Lat and came to the house to visit. In the course of our warm and reminiscing conversation, he shared how the parade had been put together. "It happened at the school," he said. His little brother was asked if he'd like to be in a parade, and he was given one of the lead flags. How proud he was.

I looked at Binh. What a fine specimen of a young man he was. I never saw him again. Twenty years later, I can hear that call, "Mrs. Moore, Mrs. Merrell, . . . over here," and with the voice, I see that beaming face.

12

The Trouble with Silence

Rosalie Beck

"I am the Lord your God; I strengthen you and tell you,
'Do not be afraid; I will help you'"
(Isa. 41:13 TEV).

Linda Pegram and I finished teaching. The night had an uneasy feel to it. The back of my neck was prickling and I wondered why.

I arrived in Vietnam in August 1973, to work as a missionary in the seacoast city of Qui Nhon. One of my major assignments was to teach English as a Second Language (ESL). Fluency in English spelled advancement to the Vietnamese; our classes filled quickly. This evening Linda and I both taught two classes, especially struggling with the Vietnamese students' pronunciation of the English "th." But a sense of strangeness permeated the air.

Early in the evening, automatic weapon fire erupted at the corner in the next block. Weapons firing during the day held no surprise for me, but the firing usually caused a flurry among the students for a few minutes. The close proximity of the military action was not causing the unrest. Something else was operating. As Linda and I walked back to our apartments, we spoke in subdued voices, glancing over our shoulders often peering into shadows warily. But we could not label our fear.

As we relaxed on the patio of my apartment, sipping limeade drinks, we discussed our nervousness. Neither of us had fragile nerves and had weathered close rifle fire and the interminable delays and frights that war brought to life in Vietnam. We had encountered dead bodies and live prisoners. But something was different.

We fell silent, finally. I gazed out over the schoolyard next to my apartment. The night was so silent. I turned to Linda at the same moment she turned to me, and we both blurted out, "The guns!!!" Now, about three miles from Qui Nhon, a village named Ba Gi housed an artillery battery of 107 howitzer cannons. The shells of those arms could travel more than 15 miles through the sky and land with deadly accuracy. The concussion from their firing echoed over the countryside. Tonight, for some reason and for the first time since I arrived in Qui Nhon, the guns were not firing. Only the normal city sounds filtered through the air. I had grown accustomed to the firing of massive weapons as a normal part of night sounds. The sudden absence of the war's ongoingness had produced our restlessness, our suspicion.

That evening I reflected: *I could become accustomed to any new thing. Would I always strain for the noise of war? Would I ever be able to trust silence again?* The human spirit is sturdy. I have grown to embrace silence, to treasure it. But for a few hours that night in 1973, silence bred unease and fear.

13

Trust

Betty J. Merrell

"When I am afraid, O Lord Almighty, I put my trust in you" (Psalm 56:3 TEV).

Fall 1965, Da Lat, South Vietnam. For nearly two years we felt God at work in our lives in Da Lat. American involvement in the war had changed. The few military advisers had multiplied into thousands of GIs landing from planes and carriers. American military families departed for the US under order of the US government.

Missionaries in our station voted by secret ballot to go or stay; the vote was unanimous to stay. Before long, the situation had worsened. Those same families stood at the military airstrip and waved good-bye to their school-aged children boarding military planes that would transfer all American students in the missionary-run school to Thailand. The daily gathering of a number of American children in one location in Vietnam did not seem wise any longer. Perhaps prayer did not make the good-bye easier for those families; it did make it possible.

The Vietnamese were coping with changing faces also. The rest-and-recuperation city of Da Lat was no longer the declared peace zone for both sides. The war moved closer to Da Lat on land and in the air. Ground mortars suddenly pierced the quiet of our nights. Planes droned overhead by day, ever searching for Vietcong staked out in the thick underbrush of the lush mountainsides, hoping to abort their nightly strikes on airstrips and ammunition dumps.

We stood at a bedroom window in the home of another family and watched the first search-and-destroy mission amid the thickness of the jungled forests surrounding Da Lat. Our eyes followed the low dives for the close look, the soaring and circling while reassessing, eventually the find and the return for the strike.

I turned my gaze to the five sons of our two families, aged 6 and under.

Each boy stood calmly watching, imitating the behavior of his parents. I saw the hand of each child in the hand of a parent.

"Oh, Father," I prayed, "during these new days, give us the simple faith of these children. May we, like them, place our complete trust in the source of our security. Here, take my hand."

I recalled a conversation with a 22-year-old young man in our church prior to our departure. "Mrs. Merrell, are you ready for Vietnam?" Billy probed with wise intent.

"I don't know," I responded. "I hope our days will not include some of the tests and trials I've read about in other missionary stories. I don't think I have what that would take, if that's what you mean."

"You'll have it," Billy shot back. "The Lord will give it to you when you need it. You'll see."

14

Twist with a Bias

Betty J. Merrell

"You must shine among them like stars lighting up the sky"
(Phil. 2:15*b* TEV).

Interest in Vietnam was at its peak in 1968 when we returned to the US for our first furlough. Ron and I together spoke to people in various settings over 300 times from July 1968 to July 1969.

I was at a state retreat center when a reporter came from the town nearby. After the introductory who, what, and when questions, she popped her big one: "How do you deliver a message of love in a climate of hate?"

I shared with her the warmth of the Vietnamese people. I told her of our four years of friendly acceptance of Americans by both town residents and rural refugees. "So, therefore, I have not worked in the climate of which you spoke." She asked other questions and I described experiences realistically and truthfully.

Before Friday of that week, I received a copy of the paper. The headline of the story read, "Love in a Climate of Hate."

I hated that hate sentence! Of course, there was hate in Vietnam. Just as it does with all mankind, hate resided there in feverish or simmering form. It did not reign in South Vietnam, however. Greed often breeds war; sometimes hate does too. Acts of violence follow. Someone orders them to support the greed or protect those who are victims of the greed and the violence. But the reporter could not shed her belief that Vietnam was blanketed and saturated with an aura of hate.

Our years in the stream of Vietnam's life called for partnering with skilled and compassionate ministers like ourselves in order to even make a dent in the massive need. Our partners included American servicemen who pulled teeth; headed hygiene, dental, or medical clinics for long days; dispensed food, toys, clothes, mosquito nets, or rice pots; dug wells, sprayed for rodents and disease-ridden varmints of all kinds; bought sewing machines, typewriters, and books;

taught English or other skills; played with the Vietnamese children; smiled at the elderly in a way that bought smiles in return; and shared the good news tucked away in the hearts they brought to Vietnam. All of this without knowing the spoken language of the people—they communicated the language of God's heart—love.

The portrait of Vietnam that was not hateful has not yet been told. What a pity that the world does not yet know it.

Our Exits

1

A Pillar of Cloud

Priscilla Tunnell

"During the day the Lord went in front of them in a pillar of
cloud to show them the way"
(Ex. 13:21a TEV).

The Communists were winning the war from north to south. We knew it but
we did not want to believe it. Mr. Ha, the staff, and the children of the orphanage in Cam Ranh believed it. They packed up, loaded themselves onto a bus,
and began an unbelievable journey. The enemy was north of the city.

Their story was injected into our lives when they arrived in Saigon one
afternoon at the Mission office, tired and hungry. After basic needs were
cared for, they decided to continue on down to the delta. Money for expens-
es was scraped together by missionaries and nationals and given to Mr. Ha.
Before we had word from them again, the missionaries had to leave the
country.

Some weeks later, they bought and stocked a small fishing vessel. Soon
children and staff set sail under a cover of fog. As they pulled away from the
shore, they heard behind them the sounds of war. The Lord went before them
as though once again covering his people with a pillar of cloud.

The voyage was difficult! Not far from Singapore they sat still in the water
and hoped for help. A vessel pulled alongside and the crew on board inquired
about the refugees. They could not help, they said, because "their own safety
might be compromised." As they pulled away, the staff and children began to
pray. In a little while the vessel returned and towed the boat to Singapore. And
the pillar of God reappeared.

I was speaking to a group of women gathered for prayer one morning in
one of the churches in Singapore. As we were praying for the children from
the orphanage, a man ran into the church and asked if a Mrs. Tunnell was in
attendance. He was bringing me a message from Mr. Ha. The children and staff
of the orphanage were being detained off the coast of Singapore, he said, and

the Singapore government was apprehensive about getting involved. They didn't want that boat to dock.

With the help of the Mission in Singapore, we met with Singapore's minister of defense. He allowed the orphanage entourage to disembark, but only to an island off the coast that had been used for drug offenders and prisoners at different times. The pillar moved again.

We were allowed to go see the children on a police launch. They were pale, dirty, thin, scared, and so happy to see us. Extra clothes, supplies, important papers, and many other things had long been tossed over the side of the boat to help keep it afloat. They only had what was on their backs and not much of that.

The next day Sherry Bengs, Priscilla Compher, and I had such a fun and funny time buying clothes for 108 people. Sizes and sex of the individuals really didn't seem to matter as we gathered underwear, shirts, shorts, and shoes in varying sizes. In a few days, officials were going to allow them to come into Singapore to spend the night as they prepared to fly them to America. And the pillar canopied over them.

The departure day was set. All arrangements were made. They were to fly to Switzerland and spend the night before heading to the US. Switzerland?! It's cold there this time of year! All we had bought were shirts and shorts! So on the night before departure the three of us went back to stores, in the tropics, trying to buy 108 sweaters or jackets. What a joke!

The next morning when we helped to load them on the plane we added three boxes of warm clothes. Our suggestion to Mr. Ha was, "Use the flight time to find something for each person." It must have worked because when they arrived in the cold country, each had a wrap.

Their flight ended at Fort Chaffee, Arkansas. As they disembarked, Vietnam missionaries Jim and Margaret Gayle were there to greet them. Jim had been the pastor of the church where most of them had become Christians in Cam Ranh, Vietnam. The pillar had moved ahead of them from one side of the earth to the other.

Mr. Nguyen Xuan Ha served as director of the Vietnam Baptist Orphanage at Cam Ranh. According to Prissy Tunnell, the orphans were moved lock, stock, and barrel from Fort Chaffee to Buckner Baptist Children's Home in Dallas, Texas.

2

Departure Remembered

Audrey Roberson

"When Paul finished, he knelt down with them and prayed. They were all
crying as they hugged him and kissed him good-bye. They were especially
sad because he had said that they would never see him again"
(Acts 20:36-38 TEV).

So many weighty military events were taking place in South Vietnam during
March 1975 that I could hardly comprehend their meaning. Our sources of
information were mixed with truth and rumor. Each new day decision making became more difficult for Bill and me.

Over 12 years of living in Vietnam, I had fallen in love with the place and
its people. Bill and I wanted to spend the remaining days of our usefulness in
serving the Lord among them. By March, however, it became increasingly
obvious that we probably could not remain in our adopted country for long.
Daily the newscasts brought word of the unrelenting advance of Communist
forces from the north. By the end of March, they were close to Saigon.

The precipitous events of the past several weeks had caused me to realize
that Bill, John, and I must seek a safer place to be while we still had a way of
exit. I could not think only of myself. My eight-year-old son must be given
special consideration. Every day Bill, John, and I prayed privately, with other
missionaries, and with Vietnamese Christians, asking God for wisdom to
make the right decisions about staying or leaving.

The one event which helped me to know that John and I should leave the
country was the closing of the small American school in Saigon which John
attended. Wives and children of other Baptist missionary families located outside Saigon had already left. Simultaneously, other missionary families in
Saigon were making decisions to leave. Now, we must do the same.

Herman and Dottie Hayes, missionaries in Vietnam since 1959, had come
to stay with us temporarily since they had been compelled by the military situation to leave their ministry in Can Tho. Our two families decided that

Dottie, John, and I would go to Bangkok, Thailand, to wait until the military crisis was over. Since Bangkok was the nearest foreign city out of the war zone, our plan was that Bill and Herman would remain in Saigon until the situation either improved or worsened. Until the very end we kept hoping we would be able to continue our missionary service in Vietnam.

We proceeded with our plan to leave as soon as possible. April 3 was set as our departure date; appropriate visas were secured. Each of us was torn between wanting to stay and sensing the need to go.

On the evening before our departure, the women of the Grace Baptist Church met to bid appropriate *adieus* to me and others who were leaving. This church was the first Vietnamese Baptist church organized in Vietnam and had its early beginnings in our first house in 1960-61. Though we had ministered in other places, that church had hovered close to our hearts. Bill hesitated to take me to the church for the gathering because a disturbance in the area was very close to Grace Church. Nevertheless, he took me and returned for me later.

During the meeting many good experiences of past years were remembered and thoughtful appreciation was mutually expressed. The Vietnamese women understood well why the missionaries should leave the country. Many of them vividly remembered the exodus from North Vietnam which had taken place in 1954 as the Vietnamese fled south. Some of those present had experienced personally that historic flight.

As the meeting stretched on into the night, several of the women rehearsed the treatment which some Christians who remained in North Vietnam had received. I felt both ominous apprehension and unusual courage in the gathering as those women sensed the difficulties facing them as they remained in their homeland, South Vietnam. We parted among many tears, all hoping that somehow the parting would not be for long.

The next morning the compound at the Vietnam Baptist Mission building was busy with missionaries and many Vietnamese, most of whom were already refugees. Leaving Co Hai, our helper, and her two little boys, as well as other dear friends, took formidable effort.

Feelings about doing what I felt was right and nagging feelings of guilt, leaving dear friends to a future colored boldly with uncertainty and fear, bore heavily upon my spirit.

One of our bookstore staff made the leaving more difficult—though unintentionally—as she came to the van designated to take us to the airport. Remembering Communist terror, as she said good-bye to me with tears, she kept repeating, "They will kill us, they will kill us."

The trip to Bangkok seemed interminably long, as if our jet felt as much backward pull as forward thrust, as if it were joining our resistance to departure. By April 10, it was obvious the Republic of South Vietnam was headed for capitulation with the Communist North. Bill and Herman joined us in

Bangkok exactly one week later. We waited and prayed—all we could do. The unwelcomed news reached us much too soon.

On April 30, 1975, we learned that the Saigon government had surrendered to the Communists. We all knew: a momentous chapter had been closed in our missionary service. But the nightmare of, "They will kill us, they will kill us," gripped hard its hold on us, and did not easily fade away.

3

Furlough*

Mary Humphries

"A soft answer turns away wrath"
(Prov. 15:1a NRSV).

When we returned to the US from our first term of service in Vietnam, we had a great opportunity to visit Washington, D.C., and to see many of the historic attractions of our nation's capital when Jim preached a revival in Alexandria, Virginia. He was invited to lead the Congress in its opening prayer one morning. Our children were tired and cross from lack of sleep and too much sightseeing, but we didn't want them to miss what we considered a significant event in their family history. The children and I sought obscurity with seats in the balcony of the House chamber. As Jim stood on the floor near the podium, Speaker of the House Carl Albert asked him if his family was present. Jim replied, "Mr. Speaker, they're tired and cross and have been fighting, so they are sitting in the balcony." Mr. Albert's answer was, "Sir, we're accustomed to fighting on this floor; bring them on down."

*Furlough *is the term used by foreign missionaries to designate a period of time in between terms of service outside the US when they may return to their homeland for rest, reunion, reporting, and renewal (education, contacts, etc.).*

4

Hurt

Beth Goad

"And I will be with you always, to the end of the age"
(Matt. 28:20*b* TEV).

I thought about it. The whole thing seemed so unreal. Did it really happen? Did we really go to Vietnam? We spread the map over the tabletop. Southeast Asia. Ken had bought the map so we could trace the tropical depressions as they formed and fashioned themselves into full-blown typhoons. Here we were in Manila—post-Vietnam, and it was *that* season in the Philippines again.

Manila and the typhoon trough were not what first caught my eyes though. *This map is out of date, it's still neatly divided: North Vietnam, South Vietnam,* I thought.

"Honey," I said to husband Ken, "we really were there, weren't we?"

"Yeah," he answered softly. "It's like a dream."

It seemed surreal, an aura of unreality now. Not so many months before, *nightmarish* would have been a better description. How many times did we wistfully say, "Oh! If we could just wake up and find this is just a horrible, horrible nightmare!"

But not so. No dream. No nightmare. Stark. Real. Fact. Each of us who called that tiny sliver of land on the South China Sea home experienced highly individualized reactions to the political and military fall of South Vietnam. Was the grief compounded for those with length of tenure? I can't say. I was one of the newer members of the missionary family. What I do know is that grief was what all of us waded through, veterans and greenhorns alike. How each loved that battered, backward little country and its people!

It hurt . . . to watch that country die. It hurt . . . to watch the reign of panic when the final, feeble flicker of hope sputtered out.

As I struggled with my own reactions, my thoughts wandered to Herman and Dottie Hayes, first pioneers in Baptist work in South Vietnam. At least they had 15 years here, I reasoned. Surely they could take home a sense of joy in multiple *well-dones*. But just recently they had caught a fresh vision of opportunities unmet in Vietnam. With new zeal, they had set their eyes on the future.

Now, what do they do with that vision? I wondered. Then it hit me, Dottie, Herman, and other long-termers must be dealing with a pileup of pain.

I rebounded and recounted what God had accomplished in our short 21 months. Ken and I had survived language school! And he had orchestrated the move to Saigon. Ken, as the new business administrator, had positioned himself to free those preachers from the administrative leads, and enabled them to return to the churches and ministries with the people to which God had called them.

Finally, we could celebrate completion of language school, and then, suddenly and most finally, we were out of the country as well.

Trite but true, time heals the hurt, or perhaps the Lord enables us to handle the hurt in time. And in His time, He heals the hurt. It took time to work through the toll of our grief. It took time for each of us. I daresay we all experienced recurring pain, for time cannot diminish the love for Vietnam and its people which God placed in our hearts. That is reality. And reality often hurts!

5

If You Had Not Come

Dottie Hayes

"And this Good News about the Kingdom will be preached
through all the world for a witness to all mankind"
(Matt. 24:14*a* TEV).

My thoughts often go back to that lovely woman who worked in our home.
Her name, Chi Tu, meant *number four*, but actually referred to the third-
born in her family. Our language teacher introduced her as his cousin.
When we met her we all thought, *How beautiful she is with her wonderful
smile, hair pulled back to form the bun at the neck, dressed in the long and
flowing* ao dai.* Chi Tu made friends immediately with the children and we
all knew we would love her. She moved into our home and became a part
of our family.

Chi Tu was a hard worker. I soon learned of her real drive to learn to cook.
I began to teach her how to cook American food. When I noticed she was not
following the recipe, she told me that she could not read. I began a long, slow
process of teaching her how to read using simple recipes and market lists. She
caught on fast and eventually became an excellent cook who could read—and
make an excellent piecrust!

Chi Tu came from a Buddhist background. After some months of working
in our home, she began attending worship services with us. She soon gave her
heart and life to Jesus Christ. We helped her learn to read her Bible and she
became a fruitful member of our newly organized church.

A few months before our furlough year in the US, Chi Tu helped me plan
an open house for our Vietnamese friends. She and I prepared the food for this
happy occasion. She loved parties and worked tirelessly to get everything ready.
More than 100 friends came to enjoy this new thing called an open house. They
especially enjoyed the goodies. Many used their napkins to take some back
home for the family to taste. No one understood the open house come-and-go
idea so they came and stayed all afternoon. We had many opportunities to

share Christ and His love. All of our hard work paid off 100-fold. We were tired but grateful.

The days were getting short before furlough with lots of work to do before departure date. When the day finally arrived, many friends came to the airport to see us off. Among those was our dear Chi Tu. As she hugged me good-bye, she whispered in my ear, "If you had not come to my country, I would not be a Christian." These words still linger in my heart and they were the words that took me back to Vietnam for a second term with a greater commitment to God's call in my life.

The ao dai is the dress-up combo worn by the petite Vietnamese women. It is composed of black or white, satin or silk, large-leg long pants worn under a long flowing split-sides, long-sleeved dress with a tunic top.

6

Innocence

Dottie Hayes

"Jesus grew both in body and in wisdom, gaining favor with God and men" (Luke 2:52 TEV).

Hope was a baby when we left our last pastorate to go to Vietnam. She was five when we returned to the US for our first furlough year. We returned to speak to the church. One of the sweet elderly women approached Hope with arms outstretched. "Oh, Hope. My, how you've grown. Do you remember me?"

"No," Hope replied very sweetly, and a little shyly, "but I remember your dress."

7

Jumping the Hurdles, Winning the Race

Priscilla Compher

"Let us run with determination the race that lies before us"
(Heb. 12:16 TEV).

During the fight for control of Nha Trang, a Red Cross official appeared at our house to inform us that my mother's cancer had returned and the prognosis was terminal. In the telegram, the family stated they were very concerned about our safety.

The telegram arrived in February 1968. Although our first four-year term was officially scheduled to end in May 1968, we decided I should try to return to the US as early as possible to lessen the strain on my family during this unwieldy time.

My thoughts raced. *How would I get from Nha Trang to Saigon? How could I get my passport from Saigon?* Passports were kept in the safe at the Vietnamese Baptist Mission headquarters in Saigon. *How would I get governmental clearance to leave? Would the Saigon airport still be open?*

We slept that night at the servicemen's center. An American pilot came in from Saigon. He had been given our passports by our Mission treasurer to somehow deliver to us. He was trying to get all missionary passports to missionaries in case of an emergency evacuation.

The pilot planned to return to Saigon the next morning—if we hurried. We did. I hunted winter clothes for the children from a large package given to us for distribution to needy refugees. I reasoned that we looked very needy at the moment, and in a few hours, we would indeed be refugees.

We flew to Saigon with the pilot. Offices were in turmoil when we arrived. Travel agents were not functioning properly. Somehow, Bob managed tickets and travel documents were approved. The four of us left on an international flight. When we landed in San Francisco, we read in the papers that the Saigon airport had closed for commercial flights until further notice.

Bob stayed in Nha Trang for several more months. Our first term of service in Vietnam was history.

8

Last Daze

Priscilla Compher

"Lord, have mercy on us. We have put our hope in you.
Protect us day by day and save us in times of trouble"
(Isa. 33:2 TEV).

The most fruitful time in our ministry, from our view—God knows more than we do about that—had come to pass in the first year and only year of our third term (1974-75). Yet the period presented some of our greatest challenges.

Bob became ill with infectious hepatitis. He was confined to bed for a month and had little energy for several months following. Local leadership and missionaries in Saigon teamed together to keep all worship services flowing. Our daughter Kathy assumed much responsibility for our nearly one-year-old son and for her own schooling. Her capability and willingness to help enabled me to continue in the development of the Cu Mong Christian refugee community.

In December 1974, while Bob was sickest, Kathy needed to go to the orthodontist in Saigon. She was able to fly to Saigon with a short-term volunteer missionary who had come to Qui Nhon briefly. Another missionary had offered to help her catch her return flight to Qui Nhon. I went to meet her. The day was stormy, the hours of waiting had been long. Like a mother, I began to worry.

I approached a couple of American men also waiting for the plane's arrival. I introduced myself. They grinned, and one said, "So you are the Baptist missionary family. We know about you from a captured Communist document. They claim that your family is to be killed when they control Qui Nhon." Then they invited me to their Christmas party in a few days. I stored the message in my memory, but at the moment I was more concerned about the current status of my daughter.

Finally a message. The plane had been canceled. Now, *canceled* in Vietnam could mean it was canceled preflight or in-flight. It could be canceled as it approached its destination but could not land. *Where would it go to land*, I questioned? *Or had the plane returned to Saigon and Kathy was alone in Saigon trying to decide what to do? Where was my daughter?*

I hurried home to call Saigon. The flight had been canceled in Saigon prior to flight, and Kathy was at the home of a missionary family. I felt unburdened once again.

That weekend two missionary men came from Saigon to help in the churches. The three of us attended that Christmas party. Before we left the social event, persons there again confirmed that we were on *the list* if the Communists gained control of the city.

In March 1975, we knew our ministry in Qui Nhon was ending. Yet we wanted to stay as long as possible. We determined three situations that would be our signal to leave. All three now existed. The American adviser kept hinting that we should leave, but we had planned a major baptismal celebration the last Sunday in March. We needed time to counsel those to be baptized. It seemed impossible to tear ourselves away.

About midnight of the Saturday prior to the Sunday of the scheduled baptismal service, we received a call from the vice chairman of the Mission. He informed us that we should leave as soon as possible. Very early the next morning, Bob made reservations for our family to leave on a scheduled embassy plane the following Wednesday.

On Sunday, we shared with all the congregations that we would be leaving the following Wednesday. One leader said, "You must go ahead. You will be killed. Perhaps we shall survive." Another begged us to please take with us their newborn son.

We left on the scheduled flight accompanied by most of the American intelligence personnel. The remainder of the foreigners in Qui Nhon were evacuated the following day. We prayed for the dear ones left behind, for their protection, and that they would remain faithful to their Lord.

The Comphers heard nothing about the Christians from Qui Nhon for over ten years after their departure in the spring of 1975. As Vietnam slowly began to open its door to the rest of the world, they began receiving letters. All had suffered greatly. Many went to prison; others were moved from their homes into "new economic zones." Food was scarce and disease rampant. Some died; many survived. They still continue strong in their personal faith and in their love as a community of faith.

9

Our New Names

Priscilla Tunnell

"I write to you, my children, because you know the Father"
(1 John 2:14a TEV).

The day Mark and I left Vietnam in 1975 was tough. The only thing that kept me from breaking down was remembering the stories of older missionaries who had to evacuate in earlier days. They had been able to return.

Chi Ba, our helper, our friend, our family, and fellow Christian helped me pack a few things. Then we piled up on my bed and we talked, cried, and prayed together.

She told me, "I really believe that this time our country is in real trouble and you will not be able to return." She continued, "In case we can ever write each other, you need to have Vietnamese names. I want to give you some." She pulled a little slip of paper from her pocket and explained, "The first one is yours and the second is for Ong (Mr.) Tunnell."

I asked, "How did you choose these names?"

"I have given you my mother's name and Ong Tunnell, my father's name." Stumbling through the tears, she finally finished, "Because you have been my Christian parents. I love you."

10

Post-Vietnam

Betty J. Merrell

"I do this so that everyone from one end of the world to the
other may know that I am the Lord"
(Isa. 45:6*a* TEV).

Spring 1987, Alabama, USA. "Betty Merrell? Did I hear you say you are Betty
Merrell? Well, you do not know me, but I prayed for you while you were in
Vietnam."

This introduction is a common one since we returned from South Vietnam
in 1974. I truthfully respond each time, "Yes, I know you did." I will never
know how many thousands of persons prayed for us fervently because they
knew we were in Vietnam. Nor will they, as laborers together with God, know
the results of their communications with the Almighty. In the final reckoning
day they will see parades of Vietnamese who would not have experienced
God's special joy had they not turned the beams of their prayers to the shores,
cities, and countrysides of Asia's Indochina. They, working with God, lighted
spots in that global sphere with God's great earth plan.

Actually, *their* prayers kept His plan in operation, not mine. My demand-
ing Vietnam decade was filled with my going to God and starting to carry out
His orders before He finished giving them. The immense needs clawed at our
brains, clogged our vision, and choked our breathing. There was so much to
do, so few to work, and so little time for talking. While in Vietnam I spent one
three-day period in private prayer related to a personal need. I also prayed
with other missionaries as we gathered in our meetings. Except for those occa-
sions, I did not spend my Vietnam years in long pauses for prayers. Rather
those years were spent in conversations with God along the way as I walked
among the children, the hurting, and the hungry.

I prayed as He led me up unlighted, stinking hallways, around winding,
tiny pathways between tinned refugee shacks, and up and down the aisles of
a dimmed auditorium filled with the elite minds of Vietnam's educators. We

tried to leave behind us the light of God's love to penetrate the darkness of spirit, body, and mind.

Today, though I work in Alabama, I join the numberless ranks of those who intercede for the Vietnamese people—those still in Southeast Asia and Vietnamese refugees in the US and around the world. God calls His children to pray about needs in His world. Awesome wonders await the son or daughter who accepts His invitation to pray.

11
Reflections on a Camp
Olive Allen

"The Lord is a refuge for the oppressed, a place of safety in times
of trouble. Those who know you, Lord, will trust you; you
do not abandon anyone who comes to you"
(Psalm 9:9-10 TEV).

"Operation Heartbreak" was a wonderful experience, but it was a heartbreak. Heartbreaks aren't always filled with hope, courage, or love, but this one was.

In April 1975, Vietnam came under Communist rule. Suddenly. Rapidly. Completely. I was home in Tennessee. My heart sank. Friends, fellow missionaries, Christian brothers and sisters, mothers, fathers, families—*where were they? What was happening to them?* I sat in a daze. Soon the phone rang, "Olive, this is Keith Parks.* Would you like to go to Fort Chaffee to help with the Vietnamese refugees?"

"Would I?" That was what I had been praying for.

"When?" I asked.

"Tomorrow," he answered. "You'll need to fly. There's not time to drive. You need to be there immediately because the need is great."

Questions flew through my head. "What shall I take, and how long will I be there?"

"We just don't know much," he said quietly. By 10:00 A.M. the next day I was in Fort Smith, Arkansas, not knowing where I would stay, who would meet me, or what I would do.

At 8:00 the following morning, the job started. We began a day care program in a huge one-room building, no materials, tables, or chairs, but that didn't seem to deter the children or the volunteers from the local churches. We didn't speak Vietnamese and they didn't speak English, but with the Lord as our interpreter we were able to share love and gain their trust. Some workers were helping to find places for the refugees to live. As soon as some would leave, others would arrive. Sometimes we had as many as 300 children.

Volunteers began to come from many walks of life, including some of the airline stewardesses whose planes had brought the refugees to Fort Chaffee.

The refugees were so lonely and sad. They had lost family, friends, country, way of life, a language they could understand, and just about everything familiar. But their courage was unconquered and their hope knew no end. They told their stories, tragic, heartbreaking, almost unbelievable stories. However, you could see the marks of truth in their eyes. They had lived it; therefore they knew it.

During this time I was so proud of my people, my country, my America. Volunteers came from everywhere. American servicemen and women came to help—ever kind and patient with the Vietnamese people. During their free time they played with the children. Clothes and food came by the truckloads.

My mind flew quickly to the verse, "I was a stranger, and ye took me in: Naked, and ye clothed me: I was sick, and ye visited me: I was in prison, and ye came unto me. . . . Inasmuch as ye have done it unto one of the least of these my brethren, ye have done it unto me" (Matt. 25:35b-36,40b KJV).

Operation Heartbreak became Operation Heartfelt.

Keith Parks served as president of the Foreign Mission Board, Southern Baptist Convention, in the 1970s.

Olive Allen's connection with Vietnam was a postretirement volunteer stint in which she trained apprentices in kindergarten ministries. Though she never learned the Vietnamese language, she could always communicate with the Vietnamese people.

12
The Gospel According to Mark

Mary Humphries

"If you appreciate wisdom, your father will be proud of you"
(Prov. 29:3 TEV).

Furlough is a very special time for missionaries and their families. Being reunited with family and friends, traveling to old familiar places and new ones, eating favorite foods, shopping in supermarkets and malls, worshiping in one's own language, hearing great music and preaching—all of these things make furlough a long-anticipated and unforgettable experience. It is so special that one MK (missionaries' kid) was overheard saying, "When I grow up, I'm going to be a missionary on furlough."

Because Vietnam was so much in the news every day, our furlough was spent telling the Vietnam story in churches across our state and nation. Since stories about Vietnam were heard everywhere, Jim worked very hard to develop one sermon which gave the people a true picture of missions work in Vietnam, and he preached it each time he stood in the pulpit. We often traveled with him in order to spend time together as a family. One Sunday morning, we were in a church in Memphis, Tennessee. The children and I were seated in the middle of the congregation. Jim had just begun the introduction to his sermon when Mark said in a very loud voice, "Mama, when is Daddy going to get a new sermon? This is the seventh time I've heard this one." Of course, that broke up the service. When the laughter and applause subsided enough, Jim said, "This is the last time I'm taking that kid with me when I preach."

13

The Wall Piece with a Message

Betty J. Merrell

"Pray to the owner of the harvest that he will send out workers
to gather in his harvest"
(Matt. 9:38 TEV).

When the knock came on the hotel door in Da Nang, our crates and boxes
were packed, the furniture stored. We were leaving Vietnam for one year. We
had moved into a hotel room for a day or two along with suitcases, camera,
briefcase, passports, two sons, etc. The suitcases were tight, bulging. We
would live out of them for a while, we knew. We had to find a house in the US
and something to put in it. And we'd need a car for the year. Everything we
owned was in those stored crates and boxes, or in these suitcases. We were at
the hotel awaiting our flight time to Saigon.

I opened the door and there stood Mr. Xuan, my language teacher, holding
a large, wrapped package as big as his smile. Mr. Xuan had been language
teacher to me and more than that to our work in Da Nang. He'd helped our
two missionary families with a lot of projects during our two years in Da
Nang. He hadn't accepted our faith, but he surely had helped us propagate it
with this, that, or the other we needed. Former educator and administrator,
wartime had turned Mr. Xuan toward varying endeavors to keep food on the
table for his wife and eight children. He had served as director of a school for
orphans in Da Nang and he taught Vietnamese or French on the side. I
remember him telling me how many of the taxicab drivers were teachers who
had to pick up a second job because their salaries were so low.

The story I remember most from those Mr. Xuan told me, however, was of
the day the Vietcong came to their village and buried alive its leaders and teachers in front of the people as a demonstration of their intentions to *purify* the
country. He had been a teenaged boy; and though a father of eight when he told
me the story, he still spent sleepless hours visualizing the scene over and over
again.

So there he stood at the door. I will admit that my first thought was, *Oh no, what am I going to do with that big, fat box!* I had nothing big enough to give it a home for the flight. I was about to think this will just have to stay here until our return next year when our guest opened his mouth to make his prepared speech.

"I've come to bring you a gift to take home, Mrs. Merrell." He carefully lifted off the plain brown paper and revealed a large rectangular black, lacquered and gold-leaf wall piece. "This is a piece the Vietnamese give to newlyweds," he stated grandly, as though the curator of some noble museum someplace. "Do you see the hen, rooster, and new chickens? With this piece we wish the newlyweds the blessing of many children."

I was about to protest. I had miscarried a baby during my two years in Da Nang and had decided the two sons were quite enough at 40. The linguist kept talking, ignoring my parted lips. "But I want to give you this to use with the people in your churches. Tell them that we thank them for sending missionaries to Vietnam, but tell them we need more. Mr. and Mrs. Merrell, I am depending on you to go home and reproduce many more missionaries to bring back with you when you come back to my country, yes!" He had that habit of saying a triumphal *yes* after he said something he was proud to have said, or some truth he had thought of and uttered without prompting.

"Yes!" I joined his punctuation. And yes, I made arrangements for special packaging. The hen and chickens have hung on our dining room wall in North America for 20 years, but they often go traveling with me to many speaking engagements. Why do I continue to take the message when doors seem closed? Mr. Xuan told me to.

Reentry?

___

1

Reunion

Toni Myers

"The gospel keeps bringing blessings and is spreading throughout
the world, just as it has among you ever since the day you first heard
about the grace of God and came to know it as it really is"
(Col. 1:6 TEV).

Scene One: Da Nang, July 1965
In 1965 our family of six moved to Da Nang. At that time the situation in that
area was very tense and the once sleepy port city was bursting at the seams
with both refugees from the countryside and recently-arrived American
marines. Housing was at a premium. We had no friends or contacts in the city,
but Lewis managed to find one hotel room with one bed. The children cheerfully slept on the floor several nights until an American marine loaned us
some military-type cots. We explored Da Nang while waiting to move into a
rental house.

In the back of our minds, we knew that when we moved in a house we
would need some household help. I would be homeschooling the three older
children and at that point our household goods had not arrived—meaning no
stove, so we would be cooking on charcoal. Knowing no one else in the city
to talk with, I asked the maid at the hotel if she could help me find a helper.
She said she had a cousin, but days passed by and no news of the cousin.

Finally moving day arrived. We had no car, so we called on Da Nang's only
means of public transportation—*cyclos* (pedicabs). Lewis and one child had
already left for the house. The three younger children and I had called over
two more cyclos and were getting into them, preparing to leave the hotel. At
that point the hotel maid came running up to us saying, "Wait! Wait! Here's
my cousin."

The cousin was 17 years old and had waist-length shining raven-black
hair. Upon questioning, I learned she had just come in from the countryside
and had never done household work before. I looked at her, pondering the

situation—no experience, I knew nothing about her. Then she gave me this beautiful, radiant smile. I said, "What's your name?" The reply was, "Mai Thi Tho." "Miss Tho, I'll call over another cyclo. Let's go to the house." Imagine Lewis's surprise when I arrived at the house with our new friend!

The Lord had provided literally at the last minute just the person our family needed. She cheerfully and lovingly helped us for eight years. Also she came to know Jesus as her Savior and took great pride in being one of the early members of the first Baptist church in Da Nang.

Scene Two: Da Nang, 24 Years Later
Our family left Vietnam in 1974. We did not see Co Tho again until 1989 when we made our first visit back to Da Nang. When word got to her that we were in town, she came to our hotel for a visit. I saw that same radiant smile. She insisted on making some *cha gio* (Vietnamese egg rolls) and we agreed she would bring them to our hotel two nights later.

At the appointed time, Lewis and I eagerly waited in the hotel lobby for her arrival. A commotion at the entry to the hotel heralded her arrival. In tow were her three children, a mutual friend and her two children—seven people—the *cha gio*, and an enormous pot of soup. The doorman at the hotel was aghast and said, "All those people with all that food can't come in here!" Lewis said (in Vietnamese), "That's OK, we'll go outside and eat on the sidewalk." The doorman rethought and replied, "Oh, come on!"

Our group of nine gathered in a corner of the hotel lobby. We ordered orange sodas from the hotel snack bar and had a wonderful banquet. What a joyful, precious time! The children were well-behaved and orderly, and soon the hotel employees, even the doorman, seemed to get into the spirit of the occasion, giving us broad smiles as they walked by.

We felt again that between people who truly care about each other time is not a barrier.

2

Unfinished Business

Priscilla Tunnell

"Remember, I will be with you and protect you wherever you go,
and I will bring you back to this land. I will not leave you until
I have done all that I have promised you"
(Gen. 28:15 TEV).

My eyes glanced downward through the window at the scene below. I had not
seen it for over 17 years. The plane lowered its landing gear and began to
touch down. My mind wandered backward through happy and wonderful
memories. One question lingered: Why did we have to leave? However, my
heart soared upward in thanks to God for the opportunity to return, even for
a little while, to a people I love, a country I had adopted, and a complex, beautiful, and enchanting culture. The wheels touched down and the butterflies in
my stomach took that as an invitation to fly, and fly they did.

For years people in the States had asked me, "If it is possible, do you ever
want to go back to Vietnam?" My response was always the same, "Won't take
me but 30 minutes to pack my bag and be ready." Well, it took much longer
than that just to fill out the forms to get a visa. When Gene and I were offered
the opportunity to return for a visit, it came like a miracle. Leaving Vietnam
had been heartwrenching. I didn't want to leave. I felt I had unfinished business there. Even after working at the US refugee camps, working in a resettlement office, taking three Vietnamese youth into my family, and helping a
Vietnamese church get started in Atlanta, I still felt my job was unfinished.
Maybe this time I could say hello again, or settle the good-bye for good.

We were met at the airport by Christian friends as well as government
workers making sure that our visit was flawless. Although the Saigon airport
(now Ho Chi Minh City) had a new building, the sights, sounds, and smells
so familiar came flooding in, and my mind ran back to all of the times I had
been there before.

We worshiped with our Christian friends each Sunday we were there.

Friends heard we were coming and came to Saigon from many places to see us. Women I had taught as young students in our seminary had married, and they introduced me to their families. Hugs, tears, and laughter filled the air as we recalled past times and shared all that had happened in our lives since we had last seen each other. We were still family. No matter what may have changed in the political realm, the Christian family remained intact.

I noticed many changes, some good from my perspective. Others made me uncomfortable. Gene and I traveled within the country but we were disappointed that we couldn't return to the mountain town of Da Lat where we had lived for 18 months. The most visible wounds of war on the land have begun to heal. But the people have only begun to heal and they need the hand of the Great Physician in every way.

I sat in the crowded worship services with tears welling up in my eyes, singing songs in Vietnamese, listening to prayers in their beautiful language, and straining to understand every word of a Vietnamese sermon. I asked God for some direction. Were we supposed to return to this country to work and minister when possible, or did God have another plan for us now? Was my feeling of unfinished business from Him or was it a personal yearning?

My answer did not come for almost a year. I stood in the Memphis airport waiting to welcome to the United States the same family that had welcomed us back to Vietnam ten months earlier. Suddenly, I knew that God had a plan for me and it is currently not located in Vietnam. As I have opportunity, I will go back—to visit or to work in a short-term project. I will pray for the work and the leaders there daily. I will stay informed about the relationship between that country and my country. I know God wants Vietnam to be a Christian country. I will encourage children and young people to think seriously about what God wants them to do with their lives. Hopefully one of them will take care of my "unfinished business."

At the time of this writing, at least eight missionary couples and several other individual missionary personnel have returned to South Vietnam for a visit or business. Social and medical needs have opened doors for help with projects.

Roll Call of Southern Baptist Women and Their Daughters in Vietnam: 1959-75

Name	Years in Vietnam	Current Residence
Anna Adams	1973	(Deceased)
Olive Allen	1969-74	Elizabethton, Tennessee
Frances Ho Awa	1971-73	Honolulu, Hawaii
Rosalie Beck	1973-75	Waco, Texas
Sherry Bengs (Mrs. Earl)	1967-75	Singapore, South Asia
Valerie Bengs Grant	1967-75	Webster, Texas
Linda Bobo (Mrs. Jim)	1974-75	Fort Worth, Texas
Elaine Housley Butler (Mrs. Craig)	1970-72	Stafford, Texas
Priscilla Compher (Mrs. Bob)	1963-75	Manila, Philippines
Katherine Compher Cocks	1964-75	Norman, Oklahoma
Ida Davis (Mrs. Bob)	1960-75	Athens, Texas
Cynthia Davis Tomlinson	1960-75	San Antonio, Texas
Rebecca Davis Ramirez	1960-75	Ho Chi Minh City, Vietnam
Diane Davis Casebier	1960-75	Waxahachie, Texas
Deborah Davis Lyon	1960-75	Spring, Texas
Ruth Davis Stenz	1963-75	Cleveland, Wisconsin
Margaret Fuller (Mrs. Ronald)	1966-72	(Deceased)
Maureen Fuller	1966-72	Walnut Creek, California
Ronalyn Fuller	1966-72	Rohnert Park, California
Margaret Gayle (Mrs. Jim)	1965-75	Denton, Texas
Beth Goad (Mrs. Ken)*	1972-75	Atlanta, Texas
Stephanie Goad	1972-75	Atlanta, Texas
Karen Russey Gross (Mrs. Bob)*	1969-71	Franklin, Tennessee
*JaNan Gross***		Franklin, Tennessee
Diane Gryseels	1970-72	Corpus Christi, Texas
Diane Hall	1968-70	Richmond, Virginia
Dottie Hayes (Mrs. Herman)	1959-75	Lafayette, Louisiana
Hope Hayes Hudson	1959-75	Alexandria, Louisiana
Virginia Hodge (Mrs. Aaron Eugene)	1970-71	Rising Sun, Maryland
Rachel James (Mrs. Sam)	1962-75	Midlothian, Virginia
Deborah James Winans	1962-75	Wake Forest, North Carolina
Aliene Johnson	1968	Address Unknown

Mary Kay Johnson	1965-67	Granbury, Texas
Mary Humphries	1966-73	San Marcos, Texas
(Mrs. Jim)		
Tracy Humphries Miller	1966-73	Dallas, Texas
Paulette Kellum	1971-75	Bartlett, Tennessee
(Mrs. Jimmy)		
Katherine Kellum	1971-75	Bartlett, Tennessee
Laura Kellum Chastain	1971-75	Bartlett, Tennessee
Barbara Lassiter	1973-75	Irmo, South Carolina
(Mrs. Jim)		
*Linsi Lassiter***		Irmo, South Carolina
*Nicole Lassiter***		Irmo, South Carolina
Marian Longbottom	1960-75	Waco, Texas
(Mrs. Sam)		
Lynda Longbottom Kunkel	1960-75	Weatherford, Texas
Betty J. Merrell	1964-74	Fultondale, Alabama
(Mrs. Rondal)		
Tura Miller (Mrs. Jack)	1973-75	Madras, Oregon
Celia Moore	1964-75	Beaumont, Texas
(Mrs. Peyton)		
C'Anne Moore Wofford	1964-75	Dallas, Texas
Toni Myers (Mrs. Lewis)	1960-75	Richmond, Virginia
Laura Myers Schultz	1960-75	Saint Ann, Missouri
Margaret Myers Wilson	1960-75	Glen Allen, Virginia
Cecelia Morris Oviedo	1968-69	Pleasantville, New York
Phyllis Tyler Nguyen	1972-74	Portland, Oregon
(Mrs. Tuan)		
*Jenny Lee Nguyen***		Portland, Oregon
*Jamie Lauren Nguyen***		Portland, Oregon
Linda Pegram	1972-74	Karachi, Pakistan
Audrey Roberson (Mrs. Bill)	1959-75	Shelby, North Carolina
Amelia Roberson Valentine	1959-75	Asheville, North Carolina
Nancy Roberson	1959-75	Weaverville, North Carolina
Pauline Routh	1963-72	Calapan, Philippines
(Mrs. Walter)		
Deanna Routh		Chicago, Illinois
Donna Routh Meeks		Orange City, Florida
Darlene Routh		Bahrain, Middle East
Carolyn A. Stereff	1968-70	Joplin, Missouri
Priscilla "Prissy" Tunnell	1971-75	Franklin, North Carolina
(Mrs. Gene)		
Gloria Turman (Mrs. Joe)	1968-75	Zambia, Africa

Anne Marie Turman Touliatos	1969-75	Birmingham, Alabama
Barbara Wigger	1968-71	Lilburn, Georgia
(Mrs. David)		
*Shayle Wigger***		Athens, Georgia
Pam Williams	1969-71	Baton Rouge, Louisiana

* Married since 1975.
** Born after service in Vietnam.